Wind and Sand

"We came down here for wind and sand, and we have got them."

Orville Wright at Kitty Hawk, October 18, 1900

Wilbur and Orville Wright.

National Air and Space
Museum

Wind and Sand

The Story of the Wright Brothers at Kitty Hawk

by Lynanne Wescott and Paula Degen
Foreword by Oliver Jensen

Harry N. Abrams, Inc., Publishers
New York

Library of Congress Cataloging-in-Publication Data

Wescott, Lynanne.
  Wind and sand.

    1. Aeronautics—United States—History.
2. Wright, Wilbur, 1867-1912.   3. Wright, Orville, 1871-
1948.   I. Degen, Paula.   II. Title.
TL521.W38   1984   629.13'00922   83-21501
ISBN 0-8109-0918-9 (hardcover : Harry N. Abrams)
ISBN 0-915992-29-9 (paperback : Eastern National)

An Eastern Acorn Press book
Copyright © 1983 by Eastern National Park & Monument Association

The original Wright brothers photographs and quotations from their writings in *Wind
and Sand* were organized, edited, and designed for publication under the auspices of
Eastern National Park & Monument Association. By special arrangement with Harry
N. Abrams, Inc., a hardbound edition of this book is available for general distribution.
The editorial contribution of Darlene Geis, Senior Editor of Harry N. Abrams, Inc.,
is gratefully acknowledged.

Eastern National Park & Monument Association promotes and aids the historical,
scientific, and educational activities of the National Park Service. As a nonprofit
cooperating association authorized by Congress, it makes interpretive material
available to park visitors by sale or free distribution. It also supports research,
interpretation, and conservation programs of the Service. Eastern Acorn Press is
the publishing imprint of Eastern National Park & Monument Association.

Jacket photographs: Wright State University and National Air and Space Museum.

Designed by Miho.

Produced by the Publishing Center for Cultural Resources.

Manufactured in the United States of America.

Foreword

Few great inventors have left behind them so complete and enthralling a record of their work and their thoughts, or seen their triumph ignored for so long as did the Wright brothers, the unassuming, persistent bicycle mechanics of Dayton, Ohio. The sharp clear photographs alone would be a great achievement, especially since they made them with their own hands, employing the bulky equipment of the period, on glass plates. The collection in this absorbing book, together with its extracts from the Wright diaries and letters, deals mainly with the four crucial years, from 1900 through 1903, in which they developed the world's first successful airplane. They called it a "flying machine" without comic intent, since in the usage of the day an "aeroplane" was merely a wing, a fragile, cambered, cloth-covered wooden frame. The setting is the remote, thinly-settled, windswept Outer Banks of North Carolina, near the village of Kitty Hawk and a large sand dune called "Kill Devil Hill". Odd, little-known names then, but part of history now.

There is a kind of extraordinary small-town ordinariness to these spare young heralds of the air age. In 1900 Wilbur was 33, just four years older than his brother Orville, and the enterprise we see has at first glance more the air of a youthful camping trip than of a scientific expedition. The brothers live in a tent, much beset from time to time by mosquitos, heavy winds, and blowing sand. Dressed for all the world like young businessmen, in suits, high stiff collars, and derbies, they are curiosities to the few native fishermen and the old salts from the nearby U.S. Life-Saving Service stations. In a day that preceded what is now called "sportswear," Wilbur made a concession to the job, or simply the wind, and shed his hard hat for a cloth cap in some pictures—only to shift at the same time to a dignified wing collar.

The camp, the costumes, the capricious little gliders, forever being hauled about and repaired after minor disasters, even the successful flights with the bold aeronauts staring ahead while lying prone on their stomachs—all of this often brings to mind the stills from Buster Keaton or Charlie Chaplin films. In those old comedies, as veteran movie-goers will remember, the cream of the jest invariably comes when the humble, preposterously dressed little hero—a rank amateur in whatever is afoot—confounds the proud experts, and succeeds where the greybeards and their costly apparatus fail.

So the tale unfolds with the Wrights. Many an early birdman met death, beginning with the legendary Icarus and coming down to the very real Otto Lilienthal, the German glider expert; many more met ridicule. In 1894 the noted inventor Sir Hiram Maxim spent some $200,000, a vast sum in those days, on a four-ton behemoth with many wings and a 360-horsepower engine. For a launch pad there was a wide-gauge railroad track. The wings were fixed to lift, and lift it tried to do—against fixed restraints—on its one test, which ended in heavy damage. There was no real system of controls had the contraption taken off; perhaps wisely Sir Hiram walked away, announced hypothetical success, and gave up his experiments. In October 1903, a greybeard of

9

vast prestige and funding, Prof. Samuel Pierpont Langley, head of the Smithsonian Institution, who had successfully flown models, made his bid to fly a man-carrying, steam-powered affair he called an "aerodrome," manned by an assistant variously designated as the "operator" or the "manager" by the press, who came *en masse*.

Like Maxim's, Langley's was a fixed-wing affair. It lunged off a catapult on top of a Potomac houseboat and fell straight into the river. After repairing it, the fiercely determined Langley tried again on December 8, while the world watched. Again the aerodrome plunged into the Potomac; the assistant escaped with his life again, but not Langley with his reputation. He blamed the catapult for catching a part of the machine each time; it was very likely true, but Congress nevertheless cut off funds for further attempts.

Government money was withdrawn; everyone in Washington was sure there never would be flying machines. Yet just nine days after Langley's second disaster, with no press on hand and only five witnesses—four men from the local life-saving station and a curious boy from Nag's Head—Orville Wright (Wilbur won the toss but messed up his first turn at the controls) took off with his 12-horsepower engine into the teeth of a 27-mile-per-hour wind. Struggling with the controls in the air, he kept the machine moving forward 12 seconds, advancing above the ground for some 100 feet until a strong gust plumped him down on the sand. It was bitter cold that day and the brothers had to keep warming themselves by a fire in an old carbide can (their "patent stove") while they took turns making three more flights. The last, piloted by Wilbur, who was now getting the hang of the controls, covered 852 feet in 59 seconds, ending so abruptly as to cause minor damage. Thereupon, not wishing to miss their regular Christmas at home, the brothers packed up for the long journey by foot, boat, and train. Orville wired his father the bare statistics of the day's triumph, adding, "Inform press."

Father was a man of mark in Dayton, a bishop in the United Brethren Church and no doubt entitled to a respectful hearing, but this was, if one meditates about it a moment, quite an assignment in public relations. Very little appeared in print, except a few buried items simply stating the Wrights' claims. The press had been burned too often and did not investigate, which must have been one of the great missed opportunities of the age. Nor did the U.S. Army look into the Wrights' Flyer when Wilbur, seeking support, wrote them three times in 1905. The generals had, after all, dropped $50,000 into the lost pot that financed Professor Langley.

After 1903, the Wrights, still unknown but never disheartened, spent a few years in Dayton, quietly building more sophisticated machines. They learned to fly them longer distances and for hours at a time, circling endlessly over a large rented cow pasture at the edge of town, visible at a distance to passengers on a country trolley line. And so the electric car, a popular new marvel at the time, helped bring about the first reasonably accurate press report on the wonder-working Wright brothers. That account appeared in the unlikely pages of a magazine for apiarists called *Gleanings in Bee Culture*, whose chatty publisher, a kind of cracker-barrel philosopher named A. I. Root, came by the cow pasture under the singing trolley wires when the Wrights were making the first circular flight in history. It was September 1904. "Dear friends," Root wrote for his next unhurried issue (to come out in January, 1905), "I have a wonderful story to tell you—a story that, in some respects, outrivals the Arabian Nights fables . . . God in His great mercy has permitted me to be, at least somewhat, instrumental in ushering in and introducing to the great wide world an invention that may outrank electric cars, the automobiles, and all other methods of travel . . ."

Root described the "two boys who love machinery" he found in the pasture, and gushed on: "It was my privilege, on the 20th day of September, 1904, to see the first successful trip of an airship, without a balloon to sustain it, that the world has ever made, that is, to turn the corners and come back to the starting point . . . there was not another machine equal to such a task as I have mentioned, *on the face of the earth*."

It was like a locomotive, he went on, groping for a metaphor, except that it had left the track, and had no wheels anyway, and sailed through the air on white wings with flapping propellers, and was, all in all, "the grandest sight of my life."

By 1908, with public appearances in the airshows of the time, the lonely and secret years were over. Fame, honors, and material rewards poured in on the Wrights. Modest contracts came in from the U.S. government, and greater ones from Europe, whither progress and excitement over aviation had moved. In 1912, when Wilbur at 45 tragically died of typhoid fever, he was a rich man. Though Orville, shattered by the loss of his inseparable companion, sold out the Wright business, he lived on as an elder statesman of aviation until 1948, and saw the world conquered, in both peace and war, by the descendants of his and Wilbur's little flying machines.

How does it happen that two young mechanics, with no more education than high school provided, living so far from the places where scientists congregate and learned men consult, could make such an astonishing achievement? *And all by themselves?*

In hindsight, the answer is perhaps perverse and paradoxical. The brothers' background may have been, in many respects, ideal. Theirs was a plain, God-fearing, happy family with a supportive widowed father and an intelligent sister who for some years "mothered" her two young brothers (two older ones had gone out into the world). Despite any lack of higher education, they were, as their writings in this book testify, home-educated, highly literate men, and it is just faintly possible that lack of contact with then-famous leaders in the field of aeronautics may have been not a handicap but a blessing in disguise—if only because it led them to think on their own. Wilbur and Orville, inseparable since childhood, were bachelors by choice, wedded to scientific enthusiasms. They had flown kites, followed the career of Lilienthal in the press, even written the Smithsonian for a list of books on flying; from the reply they discovered Octave Chanute's *Progress in Flying*

Machines. Later they wrote Chanute, an expert on gliding who took a fatherly interest in helping them. And, significantly, they read widely on birds and studied them in flight, especially those like the buzzard that hover effortlessly, slightly bending or warping their wings in the air currents. In 1899 the Wrights decided to build their own glilder, wrote the Weather Bureau in Washington for information about places with good steady winds, and were told about Kitty Hawk.

Does it matter that they were merely bicycle mechanics? Were not Eli Whitney and Henry Ford farm boys, Thomas A. Edison a newsboy, and George Stephenson—illiterate until he was 18—a humble mill-wright in the collieries of Newcastle? If there is any correlation between humble beginnings and final product, it is strongest in the case of the Wrights, for the basic skill in flying is balance in motion. So it is in bicycling.

In the nineteenth century, the age of steam, sheer power, the more massive the better, stood in the forefront of scientific thought. As this great era of technological development drew to a close, it was natural enough for would-be aeronauts to think in the same terms: fix one's wings with enough lift, add a strong motor, keep the weight reasonable, get in, take off. Control? Steer it, like a ship of the air. This is obviously an oversimplified view of pre-Wright thinking, but such state-of-the-art information as the brothers could find on aerodynamics did not help them very much. They set out with absolute faith in existing scientific data, were driven to doubt one thing after another, and finally, after two years of experiment, cast it all aside.

Brute power was not the answer or the most important element; instead it was control, and balance. And they went back, in effect, to the buzzard—the buzzard achieving stability in the air, warping the end of one wing downward to make it rise, up-warping the other to make it drop, leveling off, lazily turning, rising on air currents. The Wrights built similar mechanical warping into the glider wings they constructed. They learned how to link the two, stabilizing opposite moves simulta-neously, and later how to coordinate these motions with the rudder to offset the tendency of the glider to side slip or go into spins. As one result they discovered how to turn their machines and not simply fly straight into the wind. Where early glider enthusiasts had relied on shifting their own body weight, the Wrights built reliable mechanical controls and with these, after hundreds of trials with constantly improved gliders, mastered the art of flying in a device that was basi-cally unstable, which it had to be to cope in that unstable medium, the air.

The existing information on wings was wrong, the Wrights found, and so they built their own wind tunnel at home to study wings of many angles, aspects, and shapes, to observe how they performed. When they could find nothing suitable among the early gasoline engines of the time, they made their own. So it was with their propellers. Their bicycle background surfaced again as they linked the motor drive to the propel-ler hubs with sprockets and bicycle chains. There was, in sum, a kind of simple, sensible, one-two-three progression to their whole four-year epic, with only a few downhearted moments when they had to return to the drawing board. The story would never do for a play: no struggle between brothers, no romance, no villain, not even any suspense worth the name. Luck plays no role at all.

What must suffice is the real drama of these modest, wryly humorous, straightforward men, who hoped they were conferring a boon on mankind and, as Orville wrote in sorrow during World War I, thought they were giving the world "an invention which would make further wars practically impossible." That the Wrights' hope in that respect was dashed, as have been the dreams of other creators before and since, adds only poignancy to the story. The wind bloweth where it listeth, and it curls the sand around the base of the great monument to the brothers at Kitty Hawk, a memorial less to genius than to courage, persistence, and that most uncommon of all virtues, common sense.

Oliver Jensen

1900

For some years I have been afflicted with the belief that flight is possible to man. . . . I have been trying to arrange my affairs in such a way that I can devote my entire time for a few months to experiment in this field.

When Wilbur Wright wrote those words to Octave Chanute on May 13, 1900, he initiated a correspondence of more than two hundred letters, part of a rich historical record of the careers of two brothers who changed the world. Wilbur and his younger brother Orville shared the belief that man could fly, and together they worked to solve the mystery that had eluded experimenters for centuries.

Their story of discovering the principles of manned flight and inventing the first practical flying machines can best be told in their own words and pictures. As the Wrights began to delve seriously into a scientific study of flight in 1900, they also began to keep a record of their observations and activities. Their diaries and notebooks, together with letters to family members and to flight researchers of their day, like Chanute, provide a wealth of original source materials about these two men of genius.

Along with these written accounts, the Wright brothers left a remarkable pictorial record of their work. Photography was a deliberate part of their scientific research, and they carefully noted the subject, date, place, camera setting, type of negative, and other details for each photograph of their flight experiments. The Wrights were aware of both the scientific and the historical importance of this photographic record. They left over three hundred glass-plate negatives and hundreds of prints to future researchers in collections now principally at the Library of Congress in Washington, D.C. and at Wright State University in Dayton, Ohio. Most of the photographs were taken by the Wrights between 1898 and 1911 and were developed in the darkroom at their home in Dayton.

Through selections from these written and visual records, the Wright brothers tell their own story of the birth of aviation. Much of that story took place at an isolated spot on the Outer Banks of North Carolina. This book focuses on the years 1900 through 1911 and the visits the Wrights made to Kill Devil Hills, where their belief that man could fly became reality.

Their story tells of high technological achievement—of patient, methodical, brilliant research and experimentation. But their story also has a human side. Excerpts from their personal letters and diaries reveal much about the characters of these two men: their wit and good humor, their sensitivity and family devotion, their wonder at the possibility that they could indeed accomplish what trained scientists and engineers before them had not.

After all, there was nothing in their background to suggest that these two brothers from Dayton, Ohio, were destined for greatness. They were the sons of a minister of the United Brethren Church. Bishop Milton Wright and his wife, Susan Koerner Wright, moved frequently during the early years of church duties. Wilbur was born on a farm near Millville, eight miles east of New Castle, Indiana, on April 16, 1867. Orville was born in Dayton, Ohio, on August 19, 1871, in the house on

Hawthorn Street where the family finally settled. There were five other children: two older boys, Reuchlin and Lorin, and a younger girl, Katharine. A set of twins died in infancy.

Their mother died in 1889, too soon to know what would become of her sons. She had, however, already instilled in them a fascination for mechanical things and a zest for solving problems. Her understanding of the mechanical world was rare for a woman of her era.

Wilbur and Orville were curious and inventive even as children. They taught themselves more than they learned through formal schooling. Although both attended high school the full time required to earn a diploma, neither graduated from high school or attended college.

After their mother died and their older brothers had moved away, Wilbur and Orville continued to live in the family home with their father and sister. Neither of the boys married.

In 1892, they formed the moderately successful Wright Cycle Company and set up a shop near their home to repair, manufacture, and sell bicycles. During the slack winter seasons, they had spare time to devote to other interests.

Their first serious interest in the subject of aviation probably dates back to 1896, when they read about the gliding experiments of Otto Lilienthal in Germany. Lilienthal's death and the failure of other flight experiments began to stir the brothers' innate curiosity. They read what little they could find published on the subject. Then, as Orville later recalled in a court deposition:

In the spring of the year 1899 our interest in the subject was again aroused through the reading of a book on ornithology. We could not understand that there was anything about a bird that would enable it to fly that could not be built on a larger scale and used by man. At this time our thought pertained more particularly to gliding flight and soaring. If the bird's wings would sustain it in the air without the use of any muscular effort, we did not see why man could not be sustained by the same means.

[January 13, 1920]

The brothers knew that the Smithsonian Institution had an interest in studies of flight, so they wrote to request published material on the subject. In his deposition Orville testified that, "After reading the pamphlets sent to us by the Smithsonian we became highly enthusiastic with the idea of gliding as a sport."

In July 1899, Wilbur and Orville built a five-foot glider and tested it as a kite. They began to think about building an even larger glider. They decided that they would take a vacation from the bicycle business the following year and travel someplace where there would be better conditions for glider experiments.

Their curiosity steadily drove them to serious scientific investigations. They studied all they could find about previous flight theories. They studied birds. They corresponded with leading aeronautical researchers about the experiments of their day. They recognized the need to leave the drawing board and the laboratory to test out their theories in the air. Step by step, they conducted their research and experimentation until they achieved what no one else had ever achieved before—sustained, controlled, powered flight. These two bicycle mechanics from Dayton, Ohio, revolutionized the world from their camp at Kill Devil Hills, near the tiny fishing village of Kitty Hawk, North Carolina.

Orville and Wilbur Wright, men of genius, who together resolved the problem of human flight, photographed at the International Aviation Tournament on Long Island in 1910.

National Air and Space Museum, U.S. Air Force

From the time we were little children my brother Orville and myself lived together, played together, worked together and, in fact, thought together. We usually owned all of our toys in common, talked over our thoughts and aspirations so that nearly everything that was done in our lives has been the result of conversations, suggestions and discussions between us.

[Wilbur Wright, April 3, 1912]

Our first interest began when we were children. Father brought home to
us a small toy actuated by a rubber spring which would lift itself into the
air. We built a number of copies of this toy, which flew successfully. . . .
But when we undertook to build the toy on a much larger scale it failed to
work so well. The reason for this was not understood by us at the time, so
we finally abandoned the experiments. In 1896 we read . . . of the
experiments of Otto Lilienthal, who was making some gliding flights
from the top of a small hill in Germany. His death a few months later
while making a glide . . . increased our interest in the subject, and we
began looking for books pertaining to flight.

[Orville Wright, January 13, 1920]

The parlor of the Wright
home at 7 Hawthorn Street
as it appeared in about
1897. The guitar by the fireplace belonged to Orville.
The desk was Katharine's,
but Wilbur wrote much of his
correspondence there. The
brothers built the fireplace
themselves in 1892.

Wilbur in the bicycle shop at the Wright Cycle Company in 1897. The brothers built the gasoline motor that powered the lathe and drill press at the shop.

Wright State University

For the present I have but little time for aeronautical investigations, in fact I try to keep my mind off this subject during the bicycle season as I find that business is neglected otherwise. Later in the year I think I shall be able to give several months of my time. Just now I am content with trying to settle upon a general plan of operations, and find a suitable location. [Wilbur Wright to Octave Chanute, June 1, 1900]

**I chose Kitty Hawk because it seemed the place which most
clearly met the required conditions. . . . At Kitty Hawk, which
is on the narrow bar separating the Sound [Albemarle Sound]
from the Ocean, there are neither hills nor trees, so that it
offers a safe place for practice. Also the wind there is stronger
than any place near home and is almost constant. . . .**

[Wilbur Wright to his father, September 9, 1900]

Wilbur and Orville were eager to try out their theories. Anticipating the
end of their busy season in the bicycle shop, when they would be free to
travel, the Wrights began to look for a suitable location to experiment
with a man-carrying kite. Wilbur inquired of Octave Chanute on May
13, 1900: "My business requires that my experimental work be confined to the months between September and January and I would be
particularly thankful for advice as to a suitable locality where I could
depend on winds of about fifteen miles per hour without rain or too
inclement weather. I am certain that such localities are rare."

They studied national Weather Bureau records, looking not only
for an area with dependable winds, but also for flat, open country. The
reports from a station on the Outer Banks of North Carolina sounded
promising; winds in September averaged sixteen miles an hour. The
Wrights wrote to Joseph Dosher, the Weather Bureau man at the Kitty
Hawk Station, explaining the nature of the experiments they wished to
conduct, and asking about the suitability of the ground in the area.

The Wrights needed no stronger encouragement than the letter
they received in August from William Tate, postmaster at Kitty Hawk:

**Mr. J. J. Dosher of the Weather Bureau here has asked me to
answer your letter to him relative to the fitness of Kitty Hawk as
a place to practice or experiment with a flying machine, etc. In
answering I would say that you would find here nearly any type
of ground you could wish. You could for instance get a stretch
of sandy land 1 mile by five with a bare hill in center 80 feet
high not a tree or bush any where to break the evenness of the
wind current. This in my opinion would be a fine place; our
winds are always steady, generally from 10 to 20 miles velocity
per hour.**

**You can reach here from Eliz. City, N.C. (35 miles from
here) by boat direct from Manteo 12 miles from here by mail
boat every Mon., Wed. & Friday. We have telegraph communi-
cation and daily mails. Climate healthy. You could find good
place to pitch tents & get board in private family provided there
were not too many in your party; would advise you to come any
time from September 15 to October 15. Don't wait until
November. The autumn generally gets a little rough by
November.**

**If you decide to try your machine here & come I will take
pleasure in doing all I can for your convenience & success &
pleasure, & I assure you you will find a hospitable people when
you come among us.**

[William Tate to Wilbur Wright, August 18, 1900]

Kitty Hawk would be the place to test the 1900 glider!

ATLANTIC OCEAN
N
VIRGINIA
VIRGINIA BEACH
NORTH CAROLINA
ELIZABETH CITY
Kitty Hawk
Kill Devil Hills
ALBEMARLE SOUND
PAMLICO SOUND
RALEIGH BAY

Wilbur made plans to go on ahead and set up camp while Orville completed arrangements for their absence from the bicycle business. As he began his trip in September, Wilbur wrote to his father:

I am intending to start in a few days for a trip to the coast of North Carolina in the vicinity of Roanoke Island, for the purpose of making some experiments with a flying machine. It is my belief that flight is possible and while I am taking up the investigation for pleasure rather than profit, I think there is a slight possibility of achieving fame and fortune from it. It is almost the only great problem which has not been pursued by a multitude of investigators, and therefore carried to a point where further progress is very difficult. I am certain I can reach a point much in advance of any previous workers in this field even if success is not attained just at present. At any rate I shall have an outing of several weeks and see a part of the world I have never before visited. [September 3, 1900]

Wilbur may have been thinking about what flight would mean for travelers in the future as he slowly made the tedious trip east and south, first by train, then steamer, to Norfolk, then by train again to Elizabeth City, and then by small boat and fishing schooner into Kitty Hawk Bay.

No bridges connected the Outer Banks to the North Carolina mainland in those days. Kitty Hawk was an isolated fishing village of little more than a score of scattered houses. About a mile away in one direction were the Kitty Hawk lifesaving station and the weather station; about four miles in another direction, the Kill Devil lifesaving station. These occasional buildings and a cluster of sand dunes called the Kill Devil Hills were all that broke the barrenness of the narrow strip of land where the Wright brothers chose to make their first camp.

Wilbur reached Kitty Hawk on September 13, 1900, and Orville arrived eleven days later. The brothers boarded and lodged with the Tate family until October 4, when they set up their own camp about half a mile south of the village.

Wilbur had begun to work on assembling the glider as soon as he reached Kitty Hawk. The craft was designed to be eighteen feet in length, but Wilbur was unable to find spruce for the spars at either Norfolk or Elizabeth City. He had to substitute white pine, and the longest piece he could find was sixteen feet. So, he cut a two-foot section from the centers of the presewn wing coverings and spliced the halves together on Mrs. Tate's sewing machine. The work was almost finished when Orville arrived.

Looking forward to testing the machine, Wilbur wrote to his father:

I have my machine nearly finished. It is not to have a motor and is not expected to fly in any true sense of the word. My idea is merely to experiment and practice with a view to solving the problem of equilibrium. I have plans which I hope to find much in advance of the methods tried by previous experimenters. When once a machine is under proper control under all conditions, the motor problem will be quickly solved. A failure of motor will then mean simply a slow descent & safe landing instead of a disastrous fall. In my experiments I do not expect to

rise many feet from the ground, and in case I am upset there is nothing but soft sand to strike on. I do not intend to take dangerous chances, both because I have no wish to get hurt and because a fall would stop my experimenting, which I would not like at all. The man who wishes to keep at the problem long enough to really learn anything, positively must not take dangerous risks. Carelessness and overconfidence are usually more dangerous than deliberately accepted risks. I am constructing my machine to sustain about five times my weight and am testing every piece. I think there is no possible chance of its breaking while in the air. If it is broken it will be by awkward landing. . . . My machine is more simple in construction and at the same time capable of greater adjustment and control than previous machines.

I have not taken up the problem with the expectation of financial profit. Neither do I have any strong expectation of achieving the solution at the present time or possibly any time. My trip would be no great disappointment if I accomplish practically nothing. I look upon it as a pleasure trip pure and simple, and I know of no trip from which I could expect greater pleasure at the same cost. I am watching my health very closely and expect to return home heavier and stronger than I left. I am taking every precaution about my drinking water.

[September 23, 1900]

Whether Wilbur or his brother actually did return home "heavier and stronger" is not known. Their camp life was sometimes rigorous. They had to carry their water about a thousand feet over the sand to their camp. When they wanted to test their glider in free flight, they had to drag it nearly four miles south of their camp to the sand dunes and then nearly a hundred feet up the side of Big Kill Devil Hill. At the same time they were exerting such energy in walking and toting, they were not eating regular meals. Orville described their camp life with a touch of humor in a letter to his sister Katharine:

(I have just stopped a minute to eat a spoonful of condensed milk. No one down here has any regular milk. The poor cows have such a hard time scraping up a living that they don't have any time for making milk. You never saw such poor pitiable-looking creatures as the horses, hogs and cows are down here. The only things that thrive and grow fat are the bedbugs, mosquitoes, and wood ticks. This condensed milk comes in a can and is just like the cream of our homemade chocolate creams. It is intended to be dissolved in water, but as we cannot down it that way, we just eat it out of the can with a spoon. It makes a pretty good but rather expensive dessert that way). . . .

I believed I started in to tell what we eat. Well, part of the time we eat hot biscuits and eggs and tomatoes; part of the time eggs, and part tomatoes. Just now we are out of gasoline and coffee. Therefore no hot drink or bread or crackers. The order sent off Tuesday has been delayed by the winds. Will is 'most starved. But he kept crying that when we were rolling in lux-

uries such as butter, bacon, corn bread and coffee. I think he
will survive. It is now suppertime. I must scratch around and see
what I can get together. We still have half a can of condensed
milk, which amounts to six or eight teaspoonfuls.

[October 14, 1900]

Camp life must have been quite a contrast to the comforts the brothers
were used to back home in Dayton.

Nevertheless, Wilbur and Orville looked upon the adventure as a
vacation and as an opportunity for serious study of the possibility of
manned flight. The environment of Kitty Hawk suited both purposes.
Orville described some of the pleasures of the setting in a letter to his
sister:

This is a great country for fishing and hunting. The fish are so
thick you see dozens of them whenever you look down into the
water. The woods are filled with wild game. . . . At any time we
look out the tent door we can see an eagle flapping its way over
head, buzzards by the dozen . . . soaring over the hills and bay,
hen hawks making a raid on nearby chicken yards, or a fish
hawk hovering over the bay. . . . Looking off the other way to
the sea, we find the seagulls skimming the waves, and the little
sea chickens hopping about, as on one foot, on the beach, pick-
ing up the small animals washed in by the surf. . . .

A mockingbird lives in a tree that overhangs our tent, and
sings to us the whole day long. It is very tame, and perches on
the highest bough of the tree . . . and calls us up every morning. I think he crows up especially early after every big storm to
see whether we are still here; we often think of him in the night,
when the wind is shaking the top and sides of the tent till they
sound like thunder, and wonder how he is faring and whether
his nest can stand the storm. The mockingbird is the most common about here. The redbird, brown thrasher, wren, sparrow,
and dozens of birds which I do not know by name, are thick in
the woods nearest our camp.

The sunsets here are the prettiest I have ever seen. The
clouds light up in all colors in the background, with deep blue
clouds of various shapes fringed with gold before. The moon
rises in much the same style, and lights up this pile of sand
almost like day. I read my watch at all hours of the night on
moonless nights without the aid of any other light than that of
the stars shining on the canvas of the tent. [October 14, 1900]

The birds flying about the camp were not only a pleasure to the Wright
brothers, but also a subject for study. "Kitty Hawk is a splendid place
to observe soaring flight," Wilbur wrote to Octave Chanute on November 16, 1900. "I think at least a hundred buzzards, eagles, ospreys,
and hawks made their home within a half mile of our camp. We were
enabled to make a number of observations and settle conclusively to our
minds some points which have been much disputed among writers on
the soaring problem."

The surroundings of Kitty Hawk also provided the conditions they
sought for testing the glider. On windy autumn days they flew their

glider, first as a kite, without an operator, in order to measure the lift, drift, and center of pressure; and then, finally, in free flight, with one of the brothers lying prone on the lower wing and maneuvering the machine. The slopes of the Kill Devil Hills served as launch platforms for the gliding flights.

The brothers were encouraged by their successes. "Today we took the machine about a mile below camp to some small steep hills to try gliding. The wind died before we got there so all our experiments had to be made with the machine alone—no one on it. We let it up about four or five feet from the brow of the hill and then started forward over the embankment. We were greatly pleased with the results. . . ," Orville wrote to Katharine on October 18, 1900.

Before leaving camp at the end of October, the brothers made about a dozen free flights from Big Kill Devil Hill. Wilbur described them to Chanute on November 16, 1900: "Just before returning [to Dayton] we went down to the big hill which was about three miles from our camp and spent a day gliding. . . . The distance was between three and four hundred feet at an angle of one in six and the speed at landing was more than double that of starting."

Wilbur also described their glider to Chanute, who, as an experimenter in aeronautics himself, was interested in learning the details of the Wrights' tests at Kitty Hawk:

The machine we used was a double-decker with surfaces 17 ft. by 5 ft. A space eighteen inches wide was cut out of the lower surface, so the net surface was about one hundred and sixty-five feet, and the weight with operator was 190 lbs. The ribs were of ash bent to this shape.

The depth of curve was two and one half inches, or about one in twenty-three. The main crosspieces were of white pine. The forward pieces were triangular in cross section and located at the extreme front. The rear pieces were square and located about a foot from the rear edge.
An extra piece of cloth ran up over it to lessen resistance. The covering of the machine was French sateen, and it was put on bias so that no wire stays were needed to brace the surfaces diagonally. All the ribs were enclosed thus
The uprights were jointed to the surfaces with flexible hinges and the whole machine trussed the long way, that is laterally, but not in the fore-and-aft direction
We used fifteen-gauge spring steel wire. By tightening the wire "a" every other wire was tightened. The surfaces were thus left capable of torsion, and this was the method we used to maintain lateral equilibrium. We laid down flat on the lower surface and maintained fore-and-aft balance by means of a forward rudder. We used no rear rudder; and neither horizontal nor vertical tails. . . . We began experiments by testing the machine as a kite, and found that a wind of twenty-five miles would more than support it with operator on it. Our final estimate of its soaring speed was twenty-two miles. We soon found that our arrangements for working the front rudder and twisting the

planes were such that it was very difficult to operate them simultaneously. As we had neither the material nor the tools to change these so as to correct the trouble we were compelled to test them separately. Two minutes' trial was sufficient to prove the efficiency of twisting the planes to obtain lateral balance. We also found our system of fore-and-aft balancing quite effective but it was only when we came to gliding that we became positive of this. . . . We found no difficulty in maintaining fore-and-aft balance. The ease with which it was accomplished was a matter of great astonishment to us. It was so different from what the writings of other experimenters led us to expect. This may have been partly due to the steadiness of the wind, partly to the fixed position of the operator, and partly to a fortunate combination of circumstances of which we were not aware, but it is our hope that it was due to a new method of grouping our surfaces and to the particularly efficient rudder which we used.

[November 16, 1900]

Looking back a year later, in a lecture to the Western Society of Engineers, Wilbur summarized the results of their first experiments at Kitty Hawk:

Although the hours and hours of practice we had hoped to obtain finally dwindled down to about two minutes, we were much pleased with the general results of the trip, for setting out as we did, with almost revolutionary theories on many points, and an entirely untried form of machine, we considered it quite a point to be able to return without having our pet theories completely knocked in the head by the hard logic of experience, and our own brains dashed out in the bargain. Everything seemed to us to confirm the correctness of our original opinions: (1) that practice is the key to the secret of flying; (2) that it is practicable to assume the horizontal position; (3) that a smaller surface set at a negative angle in front of the main bearing surfaces, or wings, will largely counteract the effect of the fore and aft travel of the center of pressure; (4) that steering up and down can be attained with a rudder, without moving the position of the operator's body; (5) that twisting the wings so as to present their ends to the wind at different angles is a more prompt and efficient way of maintaining lateral equilibrium than shifting the body of the operator. [September 18, 1901]

Indeed, the Wrights were encouraged by the 1900 tests. They knew, however, that they had merely begun to explore the mysteries of human flight. When they closed their camp to return home to Dayton at the end of that first season, they were already making plans for building a larger glider and returning to the Kill Devil Hills the next year.

*In October my brother and myself spent a vacation of several weeks at
Kitty Hawk, North Carolina, experimenting with a soaring machine. We
located on the bar which separates Albemarle Sound from the ocean.
South of Kitty Hawk the bar is absolutely bare of vegetation and flat as a
floor, from sound to ocean, for a distance of nearly five miles, except a
sand hill one hundred and five ft. high which rises almost in its centre.
The main slope of the hill is to the northeast, which is facing the prevailing winds. The slope is one in six (9° 28'). To the north, northeast, east,
and southeast there is nothing but flat plain and ocean for a thousand
miles nearly. It is an ideal place for gliding experiments except for its
inaccessibility. The person who goes there must take everything he will
possibly need, for he cannot depend on getting any needed article from
the outside world in less than three weeks.*

[Wilbur Wright to Octave Chanute, November 16, 1900]

*View near the Wrights' Kitty
Hawk camp, 1900.*

At Kitty Hawk, which is on the narrow bar separating the Sound from the Ocean, there are neither hills nor trees, so that it offers a safe place for practice. Also the wind there is stronger than any place near home and is almost constant, so that it is not necessary to wait days or weeks for a suitable breeze. It is much cheaper to go to a distant point where practice may be constant than to choose a nearer spot where three days out of four might be wasted.

I have no intention of risking injury to any great extent, and have no expectation of being hurt. I will be careful, and will not attempt new experiments in dangerous situations. I think the danger much less than in most athletic games. [Wilbur Wright to his father, September 9, 1900]

The lifesaving station at Kitty Hawk in 1900, one of the few clusters of buildings to interrupt the barren scene.

I am staying at present with Mr. W. J. Tate, the post master at this place. He is also a notary public and was recently elected a county commissioner of Currituck Co. His occupation is fishing in the fishing season, which begins about Oct. 1st and lasts for about three months. His house is a two-story frame with unplaned siding not painted, no plaster on the walls, which are ceiled with pine not varnished. He has no carpets at all, very little furniture, no books or pictures. There may be one or two better houses here but his is much above average. You will see that there is little wealth and no luxurious living.

[Wilbur Wright to his father, September 23, 1900]

William J. Tate and his family on the porch of the Kitty Hawk post office. He and his half-brother, Dan Tate, were friends of the Wrights and often assisted in launching the gliders.

Wright State University

Speaking about money reminds me of a pretty good one Tom the fisherman got off a few days ago when I asked him who was the richest man in Kitty Hawk. "Dr. Kogswell," he replied. "How much has he?" I inquired. "Why, his brother owes him fifteen thousand dollars," and the young fisherman thought the question settled. Tom is a small chap . . . that can tell more big yarns than any kid of his size I ever saw. We took a picture of him as he came along the other day on his way home from the beach with a drum almost as large as he. The drum is a salt-water fish.

[Orville Wright to his sister, October 18, 1900]

Tom Tate, son of Dan Tate, with his drum fish. The 1900 glider is in the background.

Library of Congress

Kitty Hawk is a fishing village. The people make what little living they have in fishing. They ship tons & tons of fish away every year to Baltimore and other northern cities, yet like might be expected in a fishing village, the only meat they ever eat is fish flesh, and they never have any of that. You can buy fish in Dayton at any time, summer or winter, rain or shine; but you can't here. About the only way to get fish is to go and catch them yourself. It is just like in the north, where our carpenters never have their houses completed, nor the painters their houses painted; the fisherman never has any fish.

[Orville Wright to his sister, October 14, 1900]

Kitty Hawk Bay viewed from the 1900 camp.

Trying to camp down here reminds me constantly of those poor arctic explorers. We are living nearly the whole time on reduced rations. Once in a while we get a mess of fish, and if our stuff comes about the same time from Elizabeth City—which stuff consists of canned tomatoes, peaches, condensed milk, flour, bacon & butter—we have a big blow-out. . . . But it only lasts a day. . . . We have just appointed the Kitty Hawk storekeeper our agent to buy us anything he can get hold of, in any quantities he can get, in the line of fish, eggs, wild geese or ducks. We have had biscuits, molasses, coffee, and rice today. Tomorrow morning we will have biscuits (made without either eggs or milk), coffee, and rice. The economics of this place were so nicely balanced before our arrival that everybody here could live and yet nothing be wasted. Our presence brought disaster to the whole arrangement. We, having more money than the natives, have been able to buy up the whole egg product of the town and about all the canned goods in the store. I fear some of them will have to suffer as a result. [Orville Wright to his sister, October 18, 1900]

Wright State University

Orville outside the tent at the first Wright camp near Kitty Hawk, 1900.

About two or three nights a week we have to crawl up at ten or eleven o'clock to hold the tent down. When one of these 45-mile nor'easters strikes us you can depend on it there is little sleep in our camp for the night. . . . The wind shaking the roof and sides of the tent sounds exactly like thunder. When we crawl out of the tent to fix things outside the sand fairly blinds us. It blows across the ground in clouds. We certainly can't complain of the place. We came down here for wind and sand, and we have got them.

[Orville Wright to his sister, October 18, 1900]

But the sand! The sand is the greatest thing in Kitty Hawk, and soon will be the only thing. The site of our tent was formerly a fertile valley, cultivated by some ancient Kitty Hawker. Now only a few rotten limbs, the topmost branches of trees that then grew in this valley, protrude from the sand. The sea has washed and the wind blown millions and millions of loads of sand up in heaps along the coast, completely covering houses and forest. Mr. Tate is now tearing down the nearest house to our camp to save it from the sand. [Orville Wright to his sister, October 14, 1900]

The Wrights' 1900 camp was located about four miles north of the campsite of 1901 and later years.

We have been having a fine time, altogether we have had the machine out three different days, from 2 to 4 hours each time. Monday night and all day Tuesday we had a terrific wind blowing 36 miles an hour. Wednesday morning the Kitty Hawkers were out early peering around the edge of the woods and out of their upstairs windows to see whether our camp was still in existence. We were all right, however, and though wind continued up to 30 miles, got the machine out to give it another trial. The wind was too strong and unsteady for us to attempt an ascent in it, so we just flew it like a kite, running down a number of strings to the ground with which to work the steering apparatus. The machine seemed a rather docile thing, and we taught it to behave fairly well.

[Orville Wright to his sister, October 14, 1900]

The 1900 Wright glider flying as a kite.

In the afternoon we took the machine to the hill just south of our camp, formerly known as "Look Out Hill," but now as the "Hill of the Wreck". . . .

Well, after erecting a derrick from which to swing our rope with which we fly the machine, we sent it up about 20 feet, at which height we attempt to keep it by the manipulation of the strings to the rudder. The greatest difficulty is in keeping it down. It naturally wants to go higher & higher. When it begins to get too high we give it a pretty strong pull on the ducking string, to which it responds by making a terrific dart for the ground. If nothing is broken we start it up again. This is all practice in the control of the machine. . . .

After an hour or so of practice in steering, we laid it down on the ground to change some of the adjustments of the ropes, when without a sixteenth of a second's notice, the wind caught under one corner, and quicker than thought, it landed 20 feet away. . . .

We dragged the pieces back to camp and began to consider getting home. The next morning we had "cheered up" some and began to think there was hope of repairing it.

[Orville Wright to his sister, October 14, 1900]

The 1900 glider wrecked by the wind.

1901

**. . . if you are looking for perfect safety, you will do well to sit
on a fence and watch the birds; but if you really wish to learn
you must mount a machine and become acquainted with its
tricks by actual trial. [Wilbur Wright lecture to Western Society
of Engineers, September 18, 1901]**

The Wrights returned to Kitty Hawk on July 10, 1901, much earlier
than they went the first year. They decided to choose a new campsite
closer to the Kill Devil Hills where they would be near the best practice
area. Their new camp was about four miles south of Kitty Hawk and a
few hundred feet north of Big Kill Devil Hill. Moving their camp meant
that they would not have to carry their new, larger machine as far for
launching as before. Again the Wrights lived in a tent, but this year
they added a rough frame building to use as both a workshop and a
storage shed for the glider.

They had company in camp during much of their 1901 stay. Their
experiments the previous year had attracted the interest of Octave
Chanute, who asked the Wrights to allow two researchers, E. C. Huffaker and George Spratt, to join them for the new tests. Chanute visited
the camp for a short while during the summer as well. Wilbur wrote the
elderly Chanute to prepare him for the trip:

**We reached Kitty Hawk several days later than we expected
owing to the greatest storm in history of the place. Anemometer
cups gave way at 93 miles per hour so that is highest speed
recorded. After a dry spell of 7 weeks the storm was followed by
rains for a full week. This has delayed us beyond expectation,
both by preventing us from working at times, and especially by
compelling us to devote a large part of our time to fighting mosquitoes which are the worst at this time (owing to the rains) the
oldest inhabitant has ever experienced. You should by all means
bring with you from the North eight yards of the finest meshed
mosquito bar you can find, as the bar here is too large to keep
them off at night. Except for the mosquitoes our camp life has
been pleasant but exciting at times.**

**We expect to have our machine completed today as only a
few little details remain to be finished. [July 26, 1901]**

Camp life was difficult at times, as Orville described with his character-
istic humor in a long letter to his sister:

**This is Sunday evening, six o'clock, and I am writing this letter
while Will and Mr. Spratt are washing the dinner dishes. We did
not get up this morning till half past seven, and had breakfast at
a little after eleven, so that our dinner did not come till after
five this evening. I have been so busy that I have not at any time
had an opportunity to write, having had all the cooking to do
besides the work on the machine. We completed it yesterday
and spent the afternoon in gliding with some pretty exciting
results which I will relate "afer soon." Camping at Kill Devil is a
different thing from that at Kitty Hawk. We haven't had a
nor'easter yet, though we have been here over two weeks. In
spite of the fact that I looked forward to nor'easters last year**

42

with some fear, nothing could have been more welcome this
year, but it seems nature has been in a conspiracy with our
enemy, the mosquito.

We landed at Kitty Hawk two weeks ago Thursday evening,
one day after a 93-mile nor'easter which demolished the only
remaining piece of our last year's machine. We slept at Tate's
that night on a bed which looked very much like this from the
head end.
That's Will down in the center and that little fellow hanging on
to the side with both hands "is me." When I played out and
couldn't stand it any longer, I rolled down into the bottom and
made Will crawl up the side. The fellow in the bottom could get
along pretty comfortably, for when he was attacked by any foe
(which roams at large over most of the beds in these southern
places) he had the opportunity of slapping back, but the poor
fellow on the side was in a pretty fix, having both hands occupied, and had to endure the attacks the best he could.

The next morning we set out with all our baggage for Kill
Devil Hills, selecting our site and pitching our tent in a drench-
ing rain, which had come upon us unexpectedly but continued
all day and night. After fooling around all day inside the tent,
excepting on a few occasions when we rushed out to drive a few
more tent pegs, our thirst became unbearable, and we decided
upon driving the Webbert pump, no well where we could get
water being within a mile's distance. Well (pun), we got no well;
the point came loose down in the sand, and we lost it! Oh misery! Most dead for water and none within a mile! Excepting
what was coming from the skies. However, we decided to catch
a little of this, and placed the dishpan where the water dripped
down from the tent roof; and though it tasted somewhat of the
soap which we had rubbed on the canvas to keep it from mil-
dewing, it pretty well filled a long felt want. These troubles were
nothing in comparison to what was coming, so I will not relate
them further.

We continued our well driving all day Saturday, and Sunday spent the day in making a trip to Kitty Hawk (four miles)
and in reading. Sunday night I was taken sick and 'most died,
that is, I felt as if I did; and managed to keep Will up the best
part of the night. The next day I was all right, and we commenced work on our building. The work went along well and we
had the building done in three days. The building is a grand
institution, with awnings at both ends; that is, with big doors
hinged at the top, which we swing open and prop up, making an
awning the full length of the building at each end, and extending
out a little over the distance of the porch around our house. We
keep both ends open almost all the time and let the breezes have
full sway. These breezes, by the way, are a little stronger than
that big wind which blew the tops off the trees on our street a
few days before we left . . . and continue day and night, coming
in turn from all points of the compass.

Mr. Huffaker arrived Thursday afternoon, and with him a swarm of mosquitoes which came in a mighty cloud, almost darkening the sun. This was the beginning of the most miserable existence I had ever passed through. The agonies of typhoid fever with its attending starvation are nothing in comparison. But there was no escape. The sand and grass and trees and hills and everything was fairly covered with them. They chewed us clear through our underwear and "socks." Lumps began swelling up all over my body like hen's eggs. We attempted to escape by going to bed, which we did at a little after six. We put our cots out under the awnings and wrapped up in our blankets with only our noses protruding from the folds, thus exposing the least possible surface to attack. Alas! Here nature's complicity in the conspiracy against us became evident. The wind, which until now had been blowing over twenty miles an hour, dropped off entirely. Our blankets then became unbearable. The perspiration would roll off of us in torrents. We would partly uncover and the mosquitoes would swoop down upon us in vast multitudes. We would make a few desperate and vain slaps, and again retire behind our blankets. Misery! Misery! The half can never be told. We passed the next ten hours in a state of hopeless desperation. Morning brought a little better condition, and we attempted on several occasions to begin work on our machine, but all attempts had to be abandoned. We now thought that surely our enemy had done its worst, and we could hope for something better soon. Alas, "how seldom do our dreams come true."

The next night we constructed mosquito frames and nets over our cots, thinking in our childish error we could fix the bloody beasts. We put our cots out on the sand twenty or thirty feet from the tent and house, and crawled in under the netting and bedclothes . . . and lay there on our backs smiling at the way in which we had got the best of them. The tops of the canopies were covered with mosquitoes till there was hardly standing room for another one; the buzzing was like the buzzing of a mighty buzz saw. But what was our astonishment when in a few minutes we heard a terrific slap and a cry from Mr. Huffaker announcing that the enemy had gained the outer works and he was engaged in a hand-to-hand conflict with them. All our forces were put to complete rout. In our desperate attacks on the advancing foe our fortifications were almost entirely torn down, and in desperation, we fled from them, rushing all about the sand for several hundred feet around trying to find some place of safety. But it was of no use. We again took refuge in our blankets with the same results as in the previous night. Affairs had now become so desperate that it began to look as if camp would have to be abandoned or we perish in the attempt to maintain it.

Hope springs eternal; that is, it does the next morning when we begin to recover from the attack of the night before.

Remembering the claim of the U.S. Army that safety is in "a superior fire," we proceeded to build big fires about camp, dragging in old tree stumps which are scattered about over the sands at about a quarter mile from camp, and keeping up such a smoke that the enemy could not find us. Mr. Spratt, after getting in bed with the smoke blowing over him, before long announced that he could no longer stand the fire, and dragged his cot out into the clear air. A few minutes later he returned, saying the mosquitoes were worse than the smoke. He spent the balance of the night in retreat from mosquito to smoke and from smoke to mosquito. However, the mosquitoes this night were small in number as compared with any previous night or even our fires would probably have been of no avail. Mr. Huffaker, Will and I had passed the night in comparative comfort, but Mr. Spratt in the morning announced that that was the most miserable night he had ever passed through. Of course we explained to him what we had gone through, and that we were expecting a repetition of it every night. We nearly scared him off after the first night, but as every night since affairs have been improving, he is now a little less uneasy, and has hopes of enduring the agony a few weeks longer.

Yesterday most of the mosquitoes had disappeared and we had a fine day and wind for testing the new machine. We took it off to the Big Hill, about a thousand feet distant, and began our experiments. Our first experiments were rather disappointing. The machine refused to act like our machine last year and at times seemed to be entirely beyond control. On one occasion it began gliding off higher and higher (Will doing the gliding) until it finally came almost at a stop at a height variously estimated by Mr. Spratt and Huffaker at from 18 ft. to forty feet. This wound up in the most encouraging performance of the whole afternoon. This was the very fix Lilienthal got into when he was killed. His machine dropped head first to the ground and his neck was broken. Our machine made a flat descent to the ground with no injury to either operator or machine. On another occasion the machine made another similar performance and showed that in this respect it is entirely safe. These were the first descents ever made successfully after getting into the above mentioned predicament. The adjustments of the machine are way off. We expect to get it in good shape in the morning and make more successful attempts. Mr. Huffaker was much pleased with a long glide we made, which he considered the longest ever made, but we think at least three or four better have been made before. Some of our glides were very encouraging.

It is now after bedtime and since very few mosquitoes have shown up we are going to get a good start on them.

[July 28, 1901]

The unpredictable weather and the uncomfortable conditions in camp that summer would have been trouble enough, but the Wrights were also discouraged by the performance of their glider. The 1901 machine followed the same general configuration as the 1900 glider, but they increased the wing span to twenty-two feet and added a hip-cradle with which to operate the wing-twisting cables—the warping system that the Wrights used for lateral control. They also increased the camber, or curve, of the wing to 1-to-12, but they later found that curve to be too great and reduced it to 1-to-19.

Although some of their flights were as good or better than those of the year before, this machine fell short of their expectations. Their method of controlling equilibrium was not yet satisfactory. Furthermore, at times the glider behaved in a surprising manner, causing the Wrights to wonder if the center of pressure travels differently on curved surfaces than on plane surfaces—a theory that was contrary to scientific data compiled by other experimenters. Wilbur noted in his diary:

We have experimented safely with a machine of over 300 sq. ft. surface in winds as high as 18 miles per hour. Previous experimenters had pronounced a machine of such size impracticable to construct and impossible to manage. It is true that we have found this machine less manageable than our smaller machine of last year but we are not sure that the increased size is responsible for it. The trouble seems rather in the travel of the center of pressure. [July 30, 1901]

Despite some success in managing the larger machine, the Wrights felt they had little to show for their second season of testing. They closed camp on August 20, sooner than they had intended, and returned to Dayton. On the train ride home, a discouraged Wilbur told his brother that he thought it would be a thousand years before man ever learned to fly!

But back home, reflecting on the summer's experiments, the Wrights began to doubt the accuracy of calculations made by previous aeronautical investigators, particularly Lilienthal's air pressure tables. Having set out with absolute faith in the existing scientific data, and driven to doubt one thing after another, they finally cast it all aside. Now they would rely entirely upon the results of their two years of experiment.

That winter in Dayton, the brothers conducted extensive experiments using a wind tunnel that they devised to test different types of wing surfaces. From these experiments they compiled their own tables of figures—calculations that would enable them to design a machine which could lift itself. Although often overshadowed by the triumphs of the flying experiments at Kill Devil Hills, the tedious, systematic laboratory work performed by the Wrights during the winter of 1901 was a turning point in the history of human flight. With this new knowledge of aerodynamics, Wilbur and Orville confidently looked forward to a return to North Carolina and the testing of their data in actual gliding.

*Our experience of the previous year having shown the necessity of a suit-
able building for housing the machine, we erected a cheap frame building, 16 feet wide, 25 feet long, and 7 feet high at the eaves. As our
machine was 22 feet wide, 14 feet long (including the rudder) and about
6 feet high, it was not necessary to take the machine apart in any
way in order to house it. Both ends of the building, except the gable parts,
were made into doors which hinged above, so that when opened they
formed an awning at each end, and left an entrance the full width of the
building. [Wilbur Wright lecture to Western Society of Engineers,
September 18, 1901]*

*The Wrights added a frame
building to their 1901 camp
near Kill Devil Hills.*

When the time came to design our new machine for 1901, we decided to make it exactly like the previous machine in theory and method of operation. But . . . we decided to increase its lifting power. Accordingly, the curvature of the surfaces was increased to 1 in 12, to conform to the shape on which Lilienthal's table was based, and to be on the safe side, we decided also to increase the area of the machine from 165 square feet to 308 square feet, although so large a machine had never before been deemed controllable. . . . As our system of control consisted in a manipulation of the surfaces themselves instead of shifting the operator's body, we hoped that the new machine would be controllable, notwithstanding its great size. [Wilbur Wright lecture to Western Society of Engineers, September 18, 1901]

48

This photograph of Orville standing beside the upended 1901 glider shows the size of the new machine.

*We went into camp about the middle of July, and were soon joined by Mr.
E.C.Huffaker, of Tennessee, an experienced aeronautical investigator in
the employ of Mr. Chanute . . . and by Dr. G.A. Spratt, of Pennsylvania
. . . who has made some valuable investigations of the properties of variously curved surfaces and the travel of the center of pressure thereon.
Early in August, Mr. Chanute came down from Chicago to witness our
experiments, and spent a week in camp with us. These gentlemen, with
my brother and myself, formed our camping party, but in addition we
had in many of our experiments the valuable assistance of Mr. W.J.Tate
and Mr. Dan Tate, of Kitty Hawk. [Wilbur Wright lecture to Western
Society of Engineers, September 18, 1901]*

*Some members of the 1901
"camping party" (left to
right): Octave Chanute,
Orville Wright, E.C. Huffaker, and Wilbur Wright.*

I refer to the soaring flight, by which the machine is permanently sustained in the air by the same means that are employed by soaring birds. They spread their wings to the wind, and sail by the hour, with no perceptible exertion beyond that required to balance and steer themselves. What sustains them is not definitely known, though it is almost certain that it is a rising current in the air. But whether it be a rising current or something else, it is as well able to support a flying machine as a bird, if man once learns the art of utilizing it. [Wilbur Wright lecture to Western Society of Engineers, September 18, 1901]

Few photographs exist that show the Wright 1901 glider in free flight; this one was taken by Octave Chanute.

Afternoon spent in kite tests. Found lift of machine much less than Lilien-thal tables would indicate, reaching only about ¹/₃ as much. Found that machine at 100 lbs. would not glide at 3° or 4° on wind of less than about 23 to 25 miles per hour. Tried flying machine as kite at edge of slope of 1 in 1¹/₂ and induced it to fly in front of rope with strong upward pull. Tried same experiment with man on with similar result. . . . Center of pressure evidently traveling backward with decrease in angle. [Wilbur Wright's Diary A, July 29, 1901]

52

Wilbur (left) and Orville
flying the 1901 glider as
a kite.

This illustration shows the machine, alone, flying in a wind of 35 miles per hour on the face of a steep hill, 100 feet high. It will be seen that the machine not only pulls upward, but also pulls forward in the direction from which the wind blows, thus overcoming both gravity and the speed of the wind. We tried the same experiment with a man on it, but found danger that the forward pull would become so strong that the men holding the ropes would be dragged from their insecure foothold on the slope of the hill. So this form of experimenting was discontinued after four or five minutes' trial. [Wilbur Wright lecture to Western Society of Engineers, September 18, 1901]

Wright State University

This photograph, though out of focus, was important to the Wrights because it showed the 1901 glider advancing into the wind.

If I take this piece of paper, and after placing it parallel with the ground, quickly let it fall, it will not settle steadily down as a staid, sensible piece of paper ought to do, but it insists on contravening every recognized rule of decorum, turning over and darting hither and thither in the most erratic manner, much after the style of an untrained horse. Yet this is the style of steed that men must learn to manage before flying can become an everyday sport. . . . Now, there are two ways of learning how to ride a fractious horse: one is to get on him and learn by actual practice how each motion and trick may be best met; the other is to sit on a fence and watch the beast a while, and then retire to the house and at leisure figure out the best way of overcoming his jumps and kicks. The latter system is the safest; but the former, on the whole, turns out the larger proportion of good riders. It is very much the same in learning to ride a flying machine; if you are looking for perfect safety, you will do well to sit on a fence and watch the birds; but if you really wish to learn, you must mount a machine and become acquainted with its tricks by actual trial.
[Wilbur Wright lecture to Western Society of Engineers, September 18, 1901]

The Wright gliders were launched by two men running them forward into a good steady wind. Here Dan Tate and E.C. Huffaker assist with a launch.

The illustration shows one of these very slow glides at a time when the machine was practically at a standstill. The failure to advance more rapidly caused the photographer some trouble in aiming, as you will perceive. In looking at this picture you will readily understand that the excitement of gliding experiments does not entirely cease with the breaking up of camp. In the photographic darkroom at home we pass moments of as thrilling interest as any in the field, when the image begins to appear on the plate and it is yet an open question whether we have a picture of a flying machine, or merely a patch of open sky. [Wilbur Wright lecture to Western Society of Engineers, September 18, 1901]

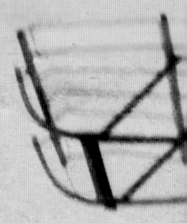

*These slow glides in rising currents probably hold out greater hope of
extensive practice than any other method within man's reach, but they
have the disadvantage of requiring rather strong winds or very large supporting surfaces. However, when gliding operators have attained greater
skill, they can, with comparative safety, maintain themselves in the air
for hours at a time in this way, and thus by constant practice so increase
their knowledge and skill that they can rise into the higher air and
search out the currents which enable the soaring birds to transport themselves to any desired point by first rising in a circle and then sailing
off at a descending angle. [Wilbur Wright lecture to Western Society of
Engineers, September 18, 1901]*

Gliding, 1901.

*Wilbur Wright in the 1901
glider just after landing.
Skid marks from previous
landings are visible in the
foreground and behind the
glider.*

We left Kitty Hawk at daybreak Tuesday morning and reached home this (Thurs.) morning. It rained four days in succession after you left and then blew straight from the south till our departure. We saw it was a waste of time to attempt to do anything at this season of the year.
      [Wilbur Wright to Octave Chanute, August 22, 1901]

The Wrights' camp surrounded by puddles caused by frequent summer rains. Their spirits dampened as well, the brothers returned home early.

1902

While the high flights were more spectacular, the low ones were fully as valuable for training purposes. Skill comes by the constant repetition of familiar feats rather than by a few overbold attempts at feats for which the performer is yet poorly prepared. [Wilbur Wright lecture to Western Society of Engineers, June 24, 1903, describing the 1902 experiments]

A new excitement stirred the brothers as they prepared for the 1902 trip to Kitty Hawk. With the tables of air pressure they had developed from their wind tunnel tests, the Wrights believed they could calculate in advance the performance of a machine. They confidently designed a glider that was even larger than the two previous models, increasing the wing span from twenty-two to thirty-two feet. As the brothers made final preparations for their trip, Katharine described the hubbub of activity in a letter to their father, who was out of town:

. . . They . . . are talking of going next Monday. . . . They really ought to get away for a while. Will is thin . . . and nervous and so is Orv. They will be all right when they get down in the sand where the salt breezes blow etc. . . . They think life at Kitty Hawk cures all ills, you know.

The flying machine is in process of making now. Will spins the sewing machine around by the hour while Orv squats around marking places to sew. There is no place in the house to live but I'll be lonesome enough by this time next week and wish that I could have some of their racket around. . . .

[August 20, 1902]

Wilbur and Orville left Dayton that next Monday as expected, but frustrating delays kept them from beginning trials with their new machine until nearly a month later. Their camp had been badly damaged by winter storms, and it required repairs. They also decided to build an addition to accommodate their larger machine, as well as the visitors they expected to join them again this season. Wilbur wrote to Octave Chanute on September 2, 1902:

We left home on the 25th and reached Kitty Hawk at 4 P.M. on the 29th after a boat trip of 36 hours from Elizabeth City. We went into camp same evening. During the year the winds blew all the foundation, which consisted of sand, out from under the building and let the ends drop down two feet, thus giving the roof a shape like that of a dromedary's back. We were a little discouraged at first but after two days work we raised it to its original level and put foundation posts under it. We do not anticipate any further trouble from this source, and in putting up the addition will put in posts to begin with. It will probably take the balance of this week to complete our building and some improvements.

The weather so far has been very fine and mosquitoes conspicuous only from their scarcity. . . . [September 2, 1902]

The brothers furnished their quarters in "grand" style compared to the earlier camps, as Wilbur described to Katharine:

We drove our well a few days ago . . . and obtained water suit-

able for all purposes. It is the best in Kitty Hawk. We also set up our table and covered the top with white oil cloth over two thicknesses of burlap, so you see we have an up to date soft top dining table. Strict orders have been given to set nothing hot on it or anything that can discolor it. We also upholstered our dining room chairs with excelsior and burlap, and have put in other royal luxuries. So far, in addition to cookery, etc., we have exercised ourselves in the trades of carpentering, furniture making, upholstering, well driving, and will add house moving next week. [August 31, 1902]

Wilbur also described the improvements in the 1902 camp to George Spratt, who had visited the Wrights the previous year:

Everything is so much more favorable this year than last that it would be a pity to have your ideas of camp life here based on your experience of one year ago. First, we have not seen a dozen mosquitoes in the two weeks and a half we have been here. I have not seen a half dozen myself. Second, we fitted up our living arrangements much more comfortably than last year. Our kitchen is immensely improved, and then we have made beds on the second floor and now sleep aloft. It is an improvement over cots. We have put battens on the cracks of the whole building including the addition, so it is much tighter and water proof than before as well as more sand proof. Our new well goes down six or eight feet below low water mark on the ocean (about ten feet deeper than last year), and we now have good water. We also have a bicycle which runs much better over the sand than we hoped, so that it only takes about an hour to make the round trip to Kitty Hawk instead of three hours as before. There are other improvements too numerous to mention, and no Huffaker and no mosquitoes, so we are having a splendid time. [September 16, 1902]

Of course, the brothers were even more excited about the improvements they were making in the new glider. Wilbur continued his letter to Spratt:

The main thing though is a new machine. We have the two surfaces completed and the uprights in place, but the rudder is not yet quite done. It is 32′ x 5′ spreading an area of 305 sq. ft. altogether. The curvature is about 1 in 25. We had it out making some tests of its efficiency today and are very much pleased with the results of our measurements. The indications are that it will glide on an angle of about 7° to $7\frac{1}{2}$° instead of $9\frac{1}{2}$° to 10° as last year. The drift is only about $\frac{1}{8}$ of the weight. In a test for "soaring" as a kite the cords stood vertical or a little to the front on a hill having a slope of only $7\frac{1}{2}$°. This is an immense improvement over our last year's machine which would soar only when the slope was 15° to 20°, as you will remember.

Mr. Chanute is sending down two machines, one built for him by Mr. Herring, and one built by Mr. Lampson (of kite fame). He is expecting to come down himself about Oct. 1st.

Mr. Herring will come down to manipulate the Chanute machines.

At present Orville and I are alone in camp. We made arrangements before coming down, to have Dan Tate with us as soon as we were ready to begin experimenting. This is all the force we absolutely need, as we will do little measuring and photographing till later when we have more men. We do not absolutely need a fourth man, yet he would not be an incumbrance by any means, especially if he was as good a companion as I know you to be.

If you are really intending to build a large machine you ought if possible by all means to see the three machines at Kitty Hawk this year. If you find it possible to come down you will need warm clothing and plenty of bed clothes as it may get cool before you get away again.

At last, on September 19, the Wrights completed assembling the new machine and were able to begin serious testing. Wilbur reported to Chanute two days later:

We finished our machine Friday noon and have made nearly 50 glides with it, in winds varying from 4 to 8 meters. We have been very cautious and our longest glide was not much over 200 ft. In the last glide yesterday on the low hill between the large ones I made a glide of 140 feet at an angle of 7°10′ on a straight slope whose greatest inclination was 7°30′, exactly facing the wind, at a speed of about 10 miles over ground, and wind of 9 miles, a total of not over 19 miles.

[September 21, 1902]

The early tests of the new machine in 1902 were very satisfying, and the brothers were pleased with their design, which Wilbur later described to a meeting of engineers:

The 1902 pattern was a double-deck machine having two surfaces each 32 feet from tip to tip, and 5 feet from front to rear. The total area of the main surfaces was about 305 square feet. The front rudder spread 15 square feet additional, and the vertical tail about 12 square feet, which was subsequently reduced to 6 square feet. The weight was 116½ lbs. Including the operator, the total weight was from 250 to 260 lbs. It was built to withstand hard usage, and in nearly a thousand glides was injured but once. It repeatedly withstood without damage the immense strains arising from landing at full speed in a slight hollow where only the tips of the wings touched the earth, the entire weight of machine and operator being suspended between.

[Lecture to Western Society of Engineers, June 24, 1903]

The one injury to the machine mentioned in Wilbur's lecture occurred on September 23, only a few days after the brothers had begun testing the 1902 model. Orville, who was operating the glider, recorded the incident in his diary:

On my third or fourth glide with the end control loose so that it

could be used, I was sailing along smoothly without any trouble at all from the fore-and-aft control, when I noticed that one wing was getting a little too high and that the machine was slowly sliding off in the opposite direction. I thought that by moving the end control mechanism an inch or so I would bring the wing back again to its proper position and, as I was going so smoothly with no need of changing the front rudder, I attempted to make the change. The next thing I knew was that the wing was very high in the air, a great deal higher than before, and I thought I must have worked the twisting apparatus the wrong way. Thinking of nothing else than the end control . . . I threw the wing tips to their greatest angle. By this time I found suddenly that I was making a descent backwards toward the low wing, from a height of 25 or thirty feet. . . . The result was a heap of flying machine, cloth, and sticks in a heap, with me in the center without a bruise or a scratch. The experiments thereupon suddenly came to a close till the repairs can be made. In spite of this sad catastrophe we are tonight in a hilarious mood as a result of the encouraging performance of the machine both in control and in angles of flight. . . . We have come to the conclusion, now, that the cause of the sudden rise of the front of the machine is a result of the wind striking on the under side of the front rudder when the relative wind is from one side.

[Diary B, September 23, 1902]

Wilbur reported the accident in a letter to Octave Chanute, written that same evening:

We did not have the machine out except for some kite experiments on Monday, but today made probably 75 glides in a wind blowing 9 to 11 meters. . . . The usual length was 150 to 225 ft. The times were about 10 to 12 seconds for the most part, though we measured but few. In fact we have spent but little time in measurements and have consequently greatly increased the amount of practice, which we consider to be the only thing now lacking to attain soaring flight. The action of the machine is almost perfect, or rather it controls both fore-and-aft & transversely just as we wish it to; and the capacity for control if properly utilized will meet any emergency, we think. The steering to right & left is now all right, the machine always turning toward the low wing. The efficiency of the machine is fully 3° better than last year. . . .

Unfortunately we finished the day with a slight catastrophe which will delay further experiment for two or three days. My brother after too brief practice with the use of the front rudder tried to add the use of the wing-twisting arrangement also, with the result that, while he was correcting a slight rise in one wing, he completely forgot to attend to the front rudder, and the machine reared up and rose some twenty-five feet and sidled off and struck the ground on alighting on one wing tip and broke several pieces of woodwork. We hope to have repairs made in a few days. [September 23, 1902]

Looking back on the mishap sometime later, Wilbur marveled that only the machine had been injured:

From the height of nearly thirty feet the machine sailed diagonally backward till it struck the ground. The unlucky aeronaut [Orville] had time for one hasty glance behind him and the next instant found himself the center of a mass of fluttering wreckage. How he escaped injury I do not know, but afterward he was unable to show a scratch or bruise anywhere, though his clothes were torn in one place. This little misadventure which occurred almost at the very beginning of our practice with the new machine was the only thing approaching an accident that happened during these experiments, and was the only occasion on which the machine suffered any injury. The latter was made as good as new by a few days' labor, and was not again broken in any of the many hundred glides which we subsequently made with it. [Lecture describing the 1902 experiments to Western Society of Engineers, June 24, 1903]

Wilbur and Orville were certain they were on the right track with their machine. They were able to compare its performance against other glider designs that Chanute, Herring, and Spratt tested at the Wrights' camp in the autumn of 1902. Wilbur wrote to his father:

. . . Our new machine is a very great improvement over anything we had built before and over any thing any one has built. We have far beaten all records for flatness of glides as we in some cases have descended only 5 1/3 degrees from the horizontal while other machines descended from 7 1/2° to 11°.

This means that in soaring we can descend much slower, and in a power machine can fly with much less power. The new machine is also much more controlable [sic] than any heretofore built so the danger is correspondingly reduced. We are being very careful and will avoid accident of serious nature if possible. Yesterday I tried three glides from the top of the hill and made 506 ft., 504 1/2 ft., and 550 ft. respectively in distance passed over. Everything is so much more satisfactory that we now believe that the flying problem is really nearing its solution. [October 2, 1902]

While their glider performed almost perfectly most of the time, in about one glide in fifty it still acted mysteriously. Wilbur noted their attempts to determine the problem:

In several . . . glides there were disturbances of the lateral equilibrium more marked than we had been accustomed to experience with the former machines, and we were at a loss to know what the cause might be. The new machine had a much greater tip-to-tip dimension than our former machines; it also had a vertical tail while the earlier ones were tailless; and the wing tips were on a line with the center while the old machines had the tips drawn down like a gull's wings. The trouble might be due to either of these differences. We decided to begin alterations at the wing tips, and . . . made the necessary changes in the truss-

66

ing, thus bringing the tips six inches lower than the center.
[Lecture describing the 1902 experiments to Western Society
of Engineers, June 24, 1903]

The solution, however, proved to be a revision of the vertical tail.
Orville wrote in his diary on October 3, 1902: "While lying awake last
night, I studied out a new vertical rudder."

Orville's idea was to change the vertical tail from a fixed vane to a
rudder that could be moved in order to recover lateral balance or to
make a turn. Wilbur not only agreed with his brother, but he also took
the suggestion a step further by proposing that they interconnect the
rudder control wires with the wing warping so that the operator could
work both controls with a single movement. Within a few hours, the
interplay of these two remarkable minds had solved the final problem in
their system of glider control. Orville recorded the completion of the
new rudder in his diary on October 6, 1902:

**We completed the change in the vertic. tail, which we have
reduced to one surface of 6 ft. area, and which is now operated
in conjunction with the wing tips, turning toward the wing with
the smaller angle of incidence so as to give it more resistance,
and thus allow the wing with the larger angle to rise more
quickly.**

Although it was not granted until 1906, the Wrights applied for
the first of their many patents in 1903, submitting the design of their
1902 glider. Orville recorded the final dimensions in his notebook:

Final Dimensions of 1902 Glider	
Both surfaces	32 ft. 1″
Up[per] surface	5 ft.
Lower ″	4 ft. 11¾ in.
Surface to surface	4 ft. 7″
Spars, c[enter]-c[enter]	3 ft. 7″
Vert. tail	14″ X 5ft. 3½″—4′6½″
″ ″	3 ft. 6″ from back of surface to front edge of tail
Uprights:	7′8″—5′8″—4′—5′8″—7′8″
Front rudder	9 ft. X 2′7″
Back edge f[ront] rudder	3 ft. 10″ from front of surface
Front rudder complete	10¼ lbs.

Both sur[faces] & uprights & wire 87 [lbs.] (not including skids, pulleys, end
operating apparatus [or] vert. tail)
Vert. tail weighs, with wires, braces, etc., 3¾ lbs.
This leaves 15 lbs. for skids, pulleys, wire & rope, etc., for operating ends,
and sand in front edge

Uprights	⅞″ X 2″
Spars	15/16″ X 1½″
Ends (upper)	⅝″ X ¾″
″ (lower)	1″ X ¾″
Front rudder bows	¾″ X ¾″

Cent. gravity of machine approximately 18″ from front edge

[Orville Wright's Notebook C, 1902]

Satisfied that their machine was now capable of mastering the winds, the brothers began to practice even more intensely to improve their operating skills. Wilbur later wrote:

The machine seems to have reached a higher state of development than the operators. As yet we consider ourselves little more than novices in management. A thousand glides is equivalent to about four hours of steady practice, far too little to give anyone a complete mastery of the art of flying. Progress is very slow in the preliminary stages, but when once it becomes possible to undertake continuous soaring, advancement should be rapid. Under special conditions it is possible that this point is not so far away as might be supposed. Since soaring is merely gliding in a rising current it would be easier to soar in front of any hill of suitable slope, whenever the wind blew with sufficient force to furnish support, provided the wind were steady. But by reason of changes in wind velocity there is more support at times than is needed, while at others there is too little, so that a considerable degree of skill, experience, and sound judgment is required in order to keep the machine exactly in the rising current. . . .

During a period of five weeks glides were made whenever the weather conditions were favorable. Many days were lost on account of rain. Still more were lost on account of light winds. Whenever the breeze fell below six miles an hour, very hard running was required to get the machine started, and the task of carrying it back up the hill was real labor. A relative speed of at least 18 miles an hour was required for gliding, while to obtain a speed of 12 miles by running required very severe exertion. Consequently unless the wind blew in our faces with a speed of at least six miles we did not usually attempt to practice; but when the wind rose to 20 miles an hour, gliding was real sport, for starting was easy and the labor of carrying the machine back uphill was performed by the wind. On the day when the wind rose to over 16 meters a second we made more than a hundred glides with much less physical exhaustion than resulted from twenty or thirty glides on days when the wind was light. [Lecture to Western Society of Engineers, June 24, 1903, describing the 1902 experiments]

The Wrights did not keep records for all of the glides made during the 1902 season, but they estimated that they made between 700 and 1,000. They made more than 375 of those glides in the last six days of experiments alone, the longest being 622.5 feet in 26 seconds. However, according to Wilbur, they were interested in far more than making record glides:

The prime object in these experiments was to obtain practice in the management of a man-carrying machine, but an object of scarcely less importance was to obtain data for the study of the scientific problems involved in flight. Observations were almost constantly being made for the purpose of determining the

amount and direction of the pressures upon the sustaining wings; the minimum speed required for support; the speed and angle of incidence at which the horizontal resistance became least; and the minimum angle of descent at which it was possible to glide. To determine any of these points with exactness was found to be very difficult indeed, but by careful observations under test conditions it was possible to obtain reasonably close approximations. [Lecture to Western Society of Engineers, June 24, 1903, describing the 1902 experiments]

Their third season at camp had been the most pleasant so far. Perhaps nature was kinder to them than in other years, or perhaps they were becoming more accustomed to the extremes of weather on the Outer Banks. Then, too, they were living in luxurious surroundings, compared to their cramped quarters of earlier years. For whatever reasons, they rarely wrote about camp life in 1902. Only occasionally did their notes mention something that occurred in camp, such as the following entries from Orville's diary:

I put in a part of the day constructing a "death trap" for a poor mouse that has been annoying us by prowling about our kitchen shelves at nights. We are now anxiously awaiting the arrival of the "victim." [Friday, September 26, 1902]

At 11 o'clock last night I was awakened by the mouse crawling over my face. Will had advised me that I had better get something to cover my head, or I would have it "chawed" off like Guillaume Mona had by the bear. I found on getting up that the little fellow had only come to tell me to put another piece of corn bread in the trap. He had disposed of the first piece. I have sworn "vengeance" on the little fellow for this impudence and insult. . . . . [Saturday, September 27]

The smart little mouse was found dead under trunk.
[Monday, October 6]

In a later diary entry, Orville commented on a storm that shook the camp:

We went to bed last night at 7:30. About half past ten we were awakened by the swaying of the building, and found a storm raging from the north. A large bottle lying at the north end of the building began to whistle, and kept it up for the rest of the night, though I made the attempt to find it. The Weather Bureau anemometer registered 50 miles per hour. We found it exceedingly cold before morning, about what we could call a five-blanket night, and as we only had four we were compelled to suffer some. [Diary B, October 15, 1902]

For the most part, however, the brothers were preoccupied with their glider tests and the successes of the 1902 season. Orville wrote to his sister Katharine on October 23, 1902, as they prepared to close the camp:

Since Lorin was here and has probably told you all the news from camp, I haven't thought it necessary to write very often, but I don't like the idea of that roaring big supper you are going to get up for us next Wednesday night getting cold before we get there Thursday, so I write to advise postponing it to Thursday, at least, for we might possibly not get home before Friday morning. We will leave here Tuesday morning on the *Lou Willis*, but Lorin has written us that the trains have changed time, so that we do not know exactly when we can reach Dayton. Lorin will know the time we ought to arrive.

Everybody is out of camp but Will and myself. Spratt left Monday. We had a good time last week after Chanute and Herring left. The work about camp was so much easier, besides the fact that the fewer in camp the more there is for each one to eat, [and] that we had lots of time to go over to the woods botanizing and looking after birds. We went to the beach a number of times and have collected a whole bucketful of starfish besides a lot of shells and a couple of king crabs which we will bring home. Spratt is a fine fellow to be with in the woods, for he knows every bird, or bug, or plant that you are likely to run across. Lorin should have been here a little later. We didn't have a bit of time while Chanute and Herring were in camp; and the weather has been so much nicer since he left. We haven't had a rain since. The past five days have been the most satisfactory for gliding that we have had. In two days we made over 250 glides, or more than we had made all together up to the time Lorin left. We have gained considerable proficiency in the handling of the machine now, so that we are able to take it out in any kind of weather. Day before yesterday we had a wind of 16 meters per second or about 30 miles per hour, and glided in it without any trouble. That was the highest wind a gliding machine was ever in, so that we now hold all the records! The largest machine ever handled . . . the longest time in the air, the smallest angle of descent, and the highest wind!!! Well, I'll leave the rest of the "blow" till we get home.

Rations are getting low again, and we are dropping back on beans. I'm cooking up a lot of them tonight, trying to do two things at once—cooking for tomorrow and writing letters. We are running a fire all night now so as to keep warm, and have managed to keep comfortable in bed, but on one or two mornings we found it a little chilly downstairs. Well, I can't think of anything else to say until I get home, so good-bye.

[October 23, 1902]

That season the Wrights had achieved the most successful glider testing in history. They had proved the accuracy of their laboratory calculations and had learned to build and control an aircraft that could be balanced in both wind and calm. They now believed they were ready for the next step: powered flight.

The flights of the 1902 glider had demonstrated the efficiency of our system of maintaining equilibrium, and also the accuracy of the laboratory work upon which the design of the glider was based. We then felt that we were prepared to calculate in advance the performance of machines with a degree of accuracy that had never been possible with the data and tables possessed by our predecessors. Before leaving camp in 1902 we were already at work on the general design of a new machine which we proposed to propel with a motor. ["How We Made the First Flight," Flying and the Aero Club of America Bulletin, *December 1913]*

Camp in 1902, showing tent and frame building. The writing may have been added to the original photograph by one of the Wright brothers.

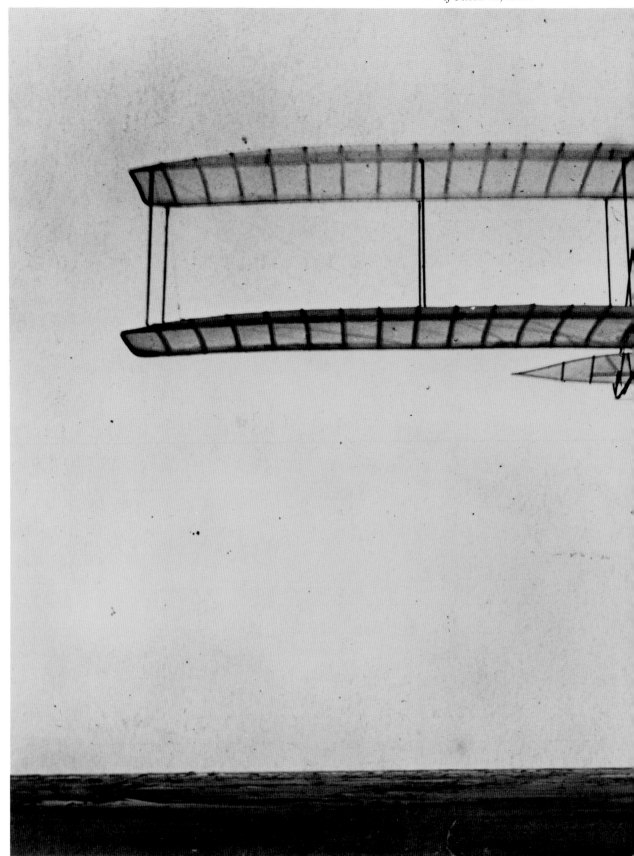

The camp building is visible below one of Wilbur's glides of October 10, 1902.

72

Wright State University

73

The practice ground at the Kill Devil Hills consists of a level plain of bare sand, from which rises a group of detached hills or mounds formed of sand heaped up by the winds. These hills are constantly changing in height and slope, according to the direction and force of the prevailing winds. The three which we use for gliding experiments are known as the Big Hill, the Little Hill and the West Hill, and have heights of 100 feet, 30 feet, and 60 feet, respectively. [Wilbur Wright lecture describing the 1902 experiments to Western Society of Engineers, June 24, 1903]

Big Kill Devil Hill in 1902.

Friday, August 29, 1902. Spent day in arranging kitchen and driving 16 ft. well. Building sank about two feet at each end. Took picture of interior of building at 10:00 A.M. 3/4 sec., 11 stop . . . .

[Orville Wright's Diary B]

The interior of the camp building, photographed on August 29, 1902, just after the Wrights arrived back at Kill Devil Hills. The 1901 glider, later dismantled, is at right.

*Saturday, September 6, 1902. Put on lath on new part of building.
Moved kitchen to new part. Built "patent" beds under roof. Saw eagle sail
out from top of Big Hill rising higher & higher till it finally sailed away.*
[Orville Wright's Diary B]

*The Wrights' "improved" and
precisely arranged kitchen
shown after the camp remod-
eling in 1902.*

*My brother & I are sleeping on special cots in the second story of our
building. We therefore have the two cots which we used last year in
reserve for visitors, &c. If you would prefer to sleep aloft as we do, suitable cots can quickly be improvised if you will bring down two yards of
heavy canvas or sailcloth (about 16 oz. would be best) for each cot. We
prefer the upper story ourselves.*

       [Wilbur Wright to Octave Chanute, September 21, 1902]

*The "patent" beds built by
the Wrights when they
remodeled their camp in
1902.*

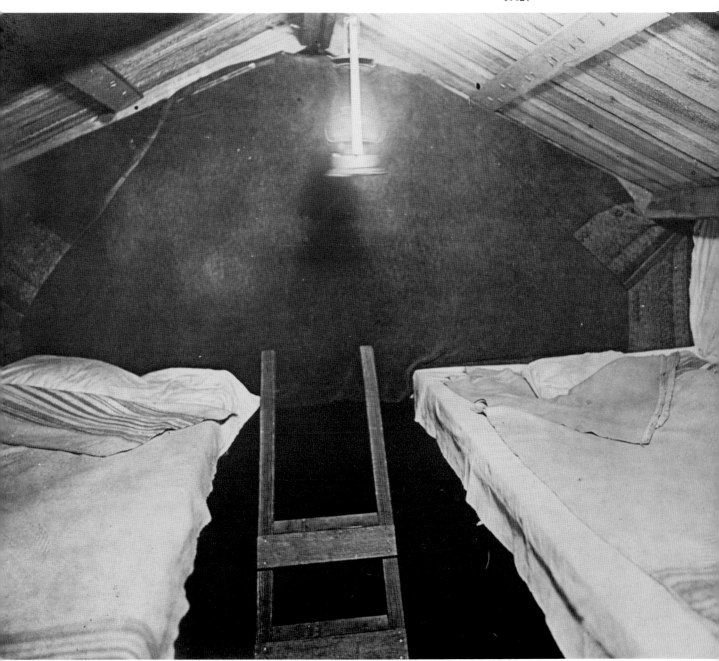

In principle soaring is exactly equivalent to gliding, the practical differ-
ence being that in one case the wind moves with an upward trend against
a motionless surface, while in the other the surface moves with a down-
ward trend against motionless air. The reactions are identical.
. . . Testing a gliding machine as a kite on a suitable slope, with just
enough wind to sustain the machine at its most favorable angle of inci-
dence, is one of the most satisfactory methods of determining its effi-
ciency. In soaring, the kite must fly steadily with the string vertical or a
little to the front. Merely darting up to this position for an instant is not
soaring.

   [Wilbur Wright lecture to Western Society of Engineers, June 24, 1903]

One of the pictures men-
tioned in Orville's diary for
September 19, 1902, shows
a side view of the glider with
Dan Tate at left and Wilbur
at right.

80

Friday, September 19, 1902. Completed the rear vertical tail at 10:30. After dinner took machine to small hill, and after taking two pictures, flying it as kite, began gliding with assistance of Dan Tate. We made no entirely free flights, but from several glides made are convinced that machine will glide on an angle of seven degrees or maybe less. Made about 25 glides during afternoon. [Orville Wright's Diary B]

Wilbur (left) and Dan Tate flying the glider.

The kite experiments having shown that it ought to be possible to glide on the 7-degree slope we next proceeded to try it. Although on this first day it was not considered advisable to venture upon any absolutely free flights, the machine soon demonstrated its ability to glide with this angle of descent. At a later period we made more than a hundred flights the full length of this slope and landed a short distance out on the level ground. On the second day the machine was taken to the Big Hill and regular gliding was commenced. [Wilbur Wright lecture to Western Society of Engineers, June 24, 1903]

Orville (left) and Dan Tate launching the 1902 glider. Wilbur is on board.

It would be well within the power of the machine to soar on the Big Hill,
which has steeper slopes, but we have not felt that our few hours of prac-
tice is sufficient to justify ambitious attempts too hastily. Before trying to
rise to any dangerous height a man ought to know that in an emergency
his mind and muscles will work by instinct rather than by conscious
effort. There is no time to think. [Wilbur Wright lecture to Western Society
of Engineers, June 24, 1903]

Orville landing the 1902
glider.

By long practice the management of a flying machine should become as instinctive as the balancing movements a man unconsciously employs with every step in walking, but in the early days it is easy to make blunders. For the purpose of reducing the danger to the lowest possible point we usually kept close to the ground. Often a glide of several hundred feet would be made at a height of a few feet or even a few inches sometimes. It was the aim to avoid unnecessary risk. [Wilbur Wright lecture to Western Society of Engineers, June 24, 1903]

One of the Wrights skimming the ground in the 1902 glider.

Although the change that had been made in the wing tips made some improvement, the lateral control still remained somewhat unsatisfactory. The tail was useful at times and at others was seriously in the way. It was finally concluded that the best way of overcoming the difficulty was by making the tail movable like a rudder. As originally built the fixed vertical tail or vane was double, but in changing to a movable rudder it was made single, as the smaller area was believed to be sufficient. As reconstructed it spread a little less than six square feet. With this improvement our serious troubles ended and thereafter we devoted ourselves to the work of gaining skill by continued practice. [Wilbur Wright lecture to Western Society of Engineers, June 24, 1903]

View of a glide off the north slope of Big Kill Devil Hill in the double-rudder machine, October 2, 1902.

A view of the 1902 glider, with the new single, movable rudder, as the machine lands within sight of the camp building.

Library of Congress

Friday, October 10, 1902. The day opened with a calm, which was followed about 7 o'clock, with a northeast wind that grew stronger & stronger as the day advanced. We took the machine to the little hill where we spent some time in practice, after which, we went to a steep slope of the big hill, where Lorin took pictures of Will gliding. . . . We went to the small hill again, and then to the second hill, where I spent most of the afternoon in practice on the end control in a wind of from seven to nine meters per second. I had great difficulty in getting started and, while trying to use the end control, caused the machine to bounce a great deal by turning the front rudder too far. Will had no trouble in the control of the machine and made a difficult glide from the top of the second hill over a course of about 280 feet, in which the wind came at great angles from one side and then the other. [Orville Wright's Diary B]

Wilbur gliding down the slope of Big Kill Devil Hill.

Wilbur gliding from the north slope of Big Kill Devil Hill. The Chanute multiple-wing glider is visible at lower left.

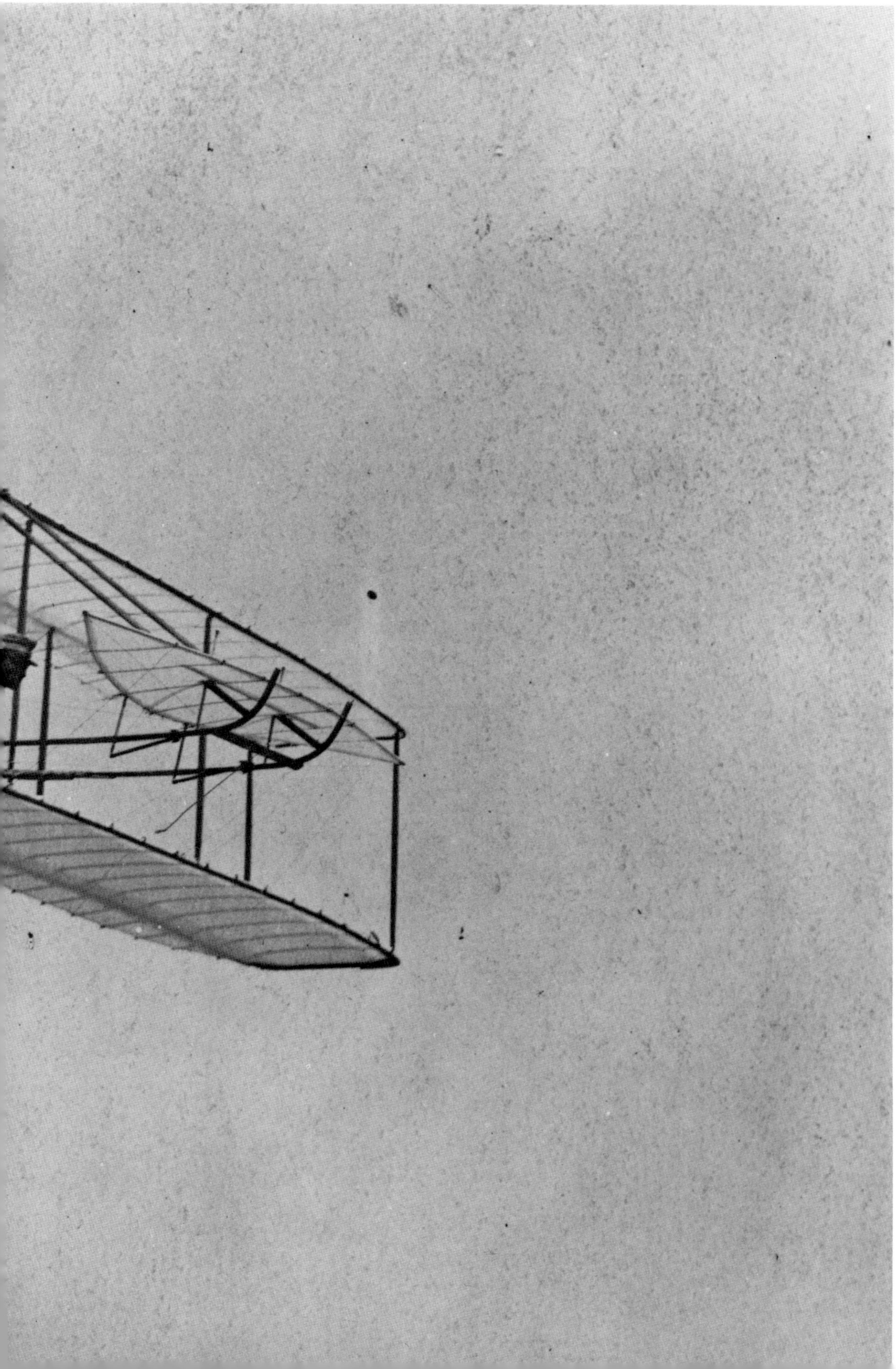

First photograph of a Wright glider making a turn.

Into the last ten days of practice we crowded more glides than in all the weeks preceding. In two days we made about two hundred and fifty, all of which were made in winds ranging from nine to sixteen and three quarters meters per second. The duration of these glides ranged from seven to sixteen seconds. This practice enabled us to very greatly increase our skill in the management of the machine. We increased our record for distance to 622¹/₂ ft., for time to 26 sec. and for angle to 5 degrees for a glide of 156 ft. We were able to make some interesting observations on the true minimum angle of descent, which we found to be about six-and-a-half degrees, and also on the speed and approximate angle of incidence of the machine while gliding at this minimum angle of descent. [Wilbur Wright to Octave Chanute, November 3, 1902]

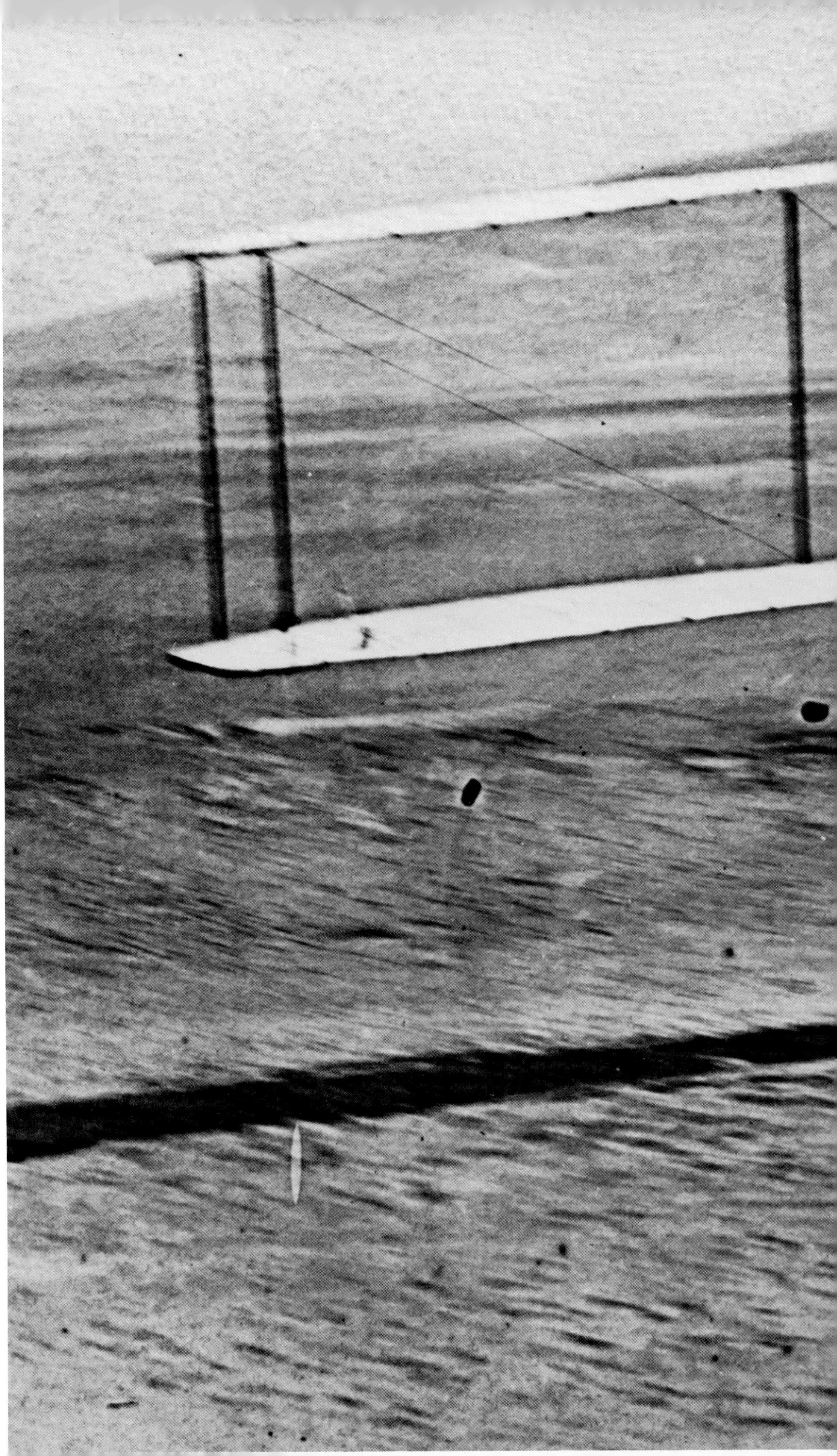

There is no question in my mind that men can build wings having as little or less relative resistance than that of the best soaring birds. The bird's wings are undoubtedly very well designed indeed, but it is not any extraordinary efficiency that strikes with astonishment but rather the marvelous skill with which they are used. . . . The soaring problem is apparently not so much one of better wings as of better operators. [Wilbur Wright lecture to Western Society of Engineers, June 24, 1903]

1903

We are expecting the most interesting results of any of our seasons of experiment, and are sure that, barring exasperating little accidents or some mishap, we will have done something before we break camp.

[Wilbur Wright to Octave Chanute, October 16, 1903]

That "something," which Wilbur referred to with restrained excitement in his letter to Chanute, that "something" would change the world permanently. Rarely in human history has a single event had such far-reaching significance for the future of mankind. That event—the world's first powered, sustained, and controlled flight—occurred during the Wrights' fourth season of flight experiments at Kill Devil Hills.

Wilbur and Orville felt certain that they were on the verge of unraveling the mysteries of human flight and fulfilling the dream of centuries. Eager to prove that their theories were correct, they must have been especially frustrated by the series of delays and disappointments that plagued them that year.

They had already been working for many months at home to achieve three requirements for their powered machine—to obtain a light, yet powerful engine; to design and build propellers that would give the needed amount of thrust; and to design and build an aircraft that would be strong enough to withstand the added weight and stress.

As early as December 1902, they had begun trying to locate a suitable gasoline engine. They wanted a motor that would produce at least eight horsepower but which would weigh no more than 200 pounds. The Wrights wrote to several automobile companies, both in the United States and abroad, to request the special manufacture of such an engine, but no company was willing to take on the assignment. As they had done so often in the past, the Wrights decided to rely upon their own resources. They enlisted the help of their mechanic at the bicycle shop, Charlie Taylor, and designed and built the engine themselves. In final form the engine, with accessories, weighed 170 pounds and gave over twelve horsepower—even more than they had hoped for.

They next had to design the propellers which, based on tables of air pressures derived from their wind tunnel experiments, would give the thrust necessary to sustain the machine in flight. Since no data on air propellers existed, they tried to adapt information about motorboat propellers. It soon became apparent, however, that the marine engineering data was inadequate for their purposes, and the Wrights were again forced to develop their own calculations. They spent several months trying to work out a coherent theory about the action of screw propellers, until they knew more than anyone had known before on the subject. They were then able to design propellers with the right diameter, pitch, and area for their needs.

The Wrights realized that they could not simply put the engine and propellers on one of their gliders. They worked out a new design that would balance the weight of the pilot against the added weight of the engine. They also attempted to reduce the risk of the engine falling on the operator in the event of accident. The new machine was their largest yet, with a wing span just over forty feet. The upper and lower wing surfaces were about six feet apart. Like the 1902 glider, the tail of the machine was movable, but the new design called for twin movable vanes instead of the single rudder. Based on their calculations for screw propellers, the Wrights designed the machine to have two propellers, attached to tubular shafts placed about ten feet apart and turning in opposite directions. They called the new machine their first "Flyer," the name they used for all their powered machines.

Early in June 1903, Orville wrote to George Spratt to report the progress they had made since Spratt had been in camp with them the year before:

Immediately after our return we began the construction of a new testing apparatus for measuring the effects of wind at various angles on surfaces. After almost completing the machine we discovered that we would have to have a very large room in which to operate it, as the current in our tunnel would be stronger on one side and then on the other, according to the course taken by the air in returning to our fan. Consequently we were compelled to lay the whole matter aside until we are able to find a more favorable place for operating. We may take it to Kitty Hawk.

We next began the designing of the ribs, spars, etc., for our next machine, on which we had decided to put a motor with propellers. We had already before leaving Kitty Hawk about decided on many of the points of construction, but it takes considerable figuring to determine the proper sizes of the different parts so as to maintain a high enough factor of safety in so large a machine. We are going to make the surfaces 40 X 6½ feet, about six feet apart. We have made up a number of the ribs, which instead of being one solid piece, as heretofore, will be built up out of two thin strips. . . .

About Christmastime we began the construction of the motor, which is of four cylinders, four-inch bore and four-inch stroke. We had estimated that we would require a little over eight horsepower to carry our weight of 625 lbs. of machine and man. At this weight we would be limited to two hundred lbs. for our motor. Our motor on completion turned out a very pleasant surprise. Instead of the eight horsepower, for which we hoped but hardly expected, it has given us 13 horsepower on the brake, with a weight of only 150 lbs. in the motor [without accessories]. During the time the engine was building we were engaged in some very heated discussions on the principles of screw propellers. We had been unable to find anything of value in any of the works to which we had access, so that we worked out a theory of our own on the subject, and soon discovered, as we usually do, that all the propellers built heretofore are *all wrong*, and then built a pair of propellers 8⅛ ft. in diameter, based on our theory, which are *all right*! (till we have a chance to test them down at Kitty Hawk and find out differently). Isn't it astonishing that all these secrets have been preserved for so many years just so that we could discover them!! Well, our propellers are so different from any that have been used before

that they will have to either be a good deal better, or a good deal worse.

    We have also made some experiments on the best shapes for the uprights of our machine, and again found out that everybody but ourselves are very badly mistaken!!! [June 7, 1903]

Finally, on September 23, the Wrights had everything in order to depart for Kitty Hawk, but they were still a long way from being able to test their new machine. Their first setback was the discovery that a winter storm had blown their building off its foundation. The brothers took the problem in stride, as is apparent in Orville's letter to his sister Katharine and Wilbur's letter to Octave Chanute, both written shortly after arrival in camp:

We reached camp Friday noon, having come over from Manteo in a small gasoline launch. We found everything in pretty good shape. The building, however, is several feet nearer the ocean than when we left last year, and about a foot lower, in places. Every year adds to our comprehension of the wonders of this place. We had supposed two years ago, when the wind at a speed of 107 mile per hour took the anemometer cups away with it (beating anything within the memory of the oldest inhabitant), and when the mosquitoes were so thick as to dim the very brightness of the sun, exceeding in numbers all excepting those that devoured the whole of Raleigh's settlers on Roanoke, and last year when lightning turned night into day, and burned down every telegraph pole between here and Kitty Hawk, we had supposed that nature had reached her limit; but far from it! Dan says this year has been one continuous succession of storms of unprecedented severity; the rain has descended in such torrents as to make a lake for miles about our camp; the mosquitoes were so thick that they turned day into night, and the lightning so terrible that it turned night into day. Really it nearly paralyzes the mind to try to think of all these things at once. Besides all these, the sun was so hot, it must have made soup of the mosquitoes and rain! Nevertheless, these sturdy Kitty Hawkers have survived it all, and are still here to welcome us among them. . . .

    We have started the new building and will probably have it pretty well up by the end of this week. We will have the old machine ready for practice on days of good winds, and will work on the new machine on rainy and calm days. The hills are in the best shape for gliding they have ever been, and things are starting off more favorably than in any year before. [Orville Wright to his sister, September 26, 1903]

We reached camp, via Manteo, at noon last Friday, and found everything all right about camp, except that a 90-mile wind last February had lifted our building off its foundation and set it over to the east nearly two feet. We made preparations to begin the erection of the new building on Monday but the conditions for gliding were so fine that we took the [old] machine out and spent the finest day we have ever had in practice. We made about 75 glides, nearly all of more than 20 seconds duration. The longest was $30^{2}/_5$ seconds which beats our former records. We did some practicing at soaring and found it easier than we expected. Once we succeeded in remaining almost in one spot for $26^{2}/_5$ seconds and finally landed fifty feet from the starting point. With a little more practice I think we can soar on the north slope of the Big Hill whenever the wind has a velocity of 9 meters or more. The wind on Monday was 11 meters at start and gradually increased to a little over 14 meters and then declined to about 9 meters.

Since Monday we have been working on the new building and hope to have it finished in a few days more. Its inside dimensions are 44″ X 16′ X 9′. [Wilbur Wright to Octave Chanute, October 1, 1903]

The new building was not quite complete when it was put to a real test by one of the worst storms to hit the Kitty Hawk region in years. Wilbur described their adventures of that day in a letter to Katharine:

"O, you ought to have seen it! You ought to have seen it! Great big sing." The trouble all came from my beginning on Sunday to predict a north wind for Thursday. But when Thursday appeared with a mere breath of air from the south my reputation as a prophet went down below that of people who set up in this business "in their own country." However about two o'clock in the afternoon a storm hove to view that made the storm that followed the prayers of Elijah look small in comparison. The wind suddenly whirled round to the north and increased to something like 40 miles an hour and was accompanied by a regular cloud burst. In this country the winds usually blow from the north, then from the east, next the south, and then from the west, and on to the north again. But when the wind begins to "back up," that is, veer from south to east and north, &c., then look out, for it means a cyclone is coming. Well, the wind backed up in such a hurry that it became dizzy or something. Maybe it got so in love with backing up that it went forward a little sometimes just to have the fun of "backing up" again. It repeated this process seven times in four days, and as it reared up every time it backed, you can imagine that there was something doing. The first night the wind was probably about 50 miles, and Orville and I lost much sleep. I suspect that in our early days we had a habit of contrariness which made us determined that the more they rocked us, the more we would not go to sleep. I can not otherwise account for having such a habit now. It is really an unfortunate habit in this climate. As the new building was not quite complete as to bracing, &c., we expected it to go first, so we lay there rocking on the billows waiting to hear it crash. Toward morning we could hear the water sloshing around on the floor of our old building, technically called the "Summer house," the new building being called the "hand car," a corruption of the French "hangar" used by foreign airship men. Orville got up to investigate (he being the expert on night alarms at home, you know), and reported the floor under water at the north end, but the south end embracing the kitchen, library, &c., still dry, "And the evening and the morning were the first day."

The second day opened with the gale still continuing with a steady drizzling rain. The wind veered from the north west to the north during the morning and dropped to about 30 miles, but after dinner it began to back up again. We set to work "tooth and nail" (using a hammer instead of our teeth however) putting braces inside our new building. The climax came about 4 o'clock when the wind reached 75 miles an hour. Suddenly a corner of our tar-paper roof gave way under the pressure and we saw that if the trouble were not stopped the whole roof would probably go. Orville put on my heavy over coat, and grabbing the ladder sallied forth from the south end of the building. At first it appeared that he was going down to repair some of the rents in the Big Hill which was being badly torn to pieces, for he began by walking backwards about 50 feet. After a while I saw him come back past the side opening in our partially raised awning door. The annexed woodcut shows the situation at this time.  The wings on his back are the tails of my overcoat. The big mosquito-like images just above him are imaginary trees being bent over by the force of the wind. Thereupon I sallied out to help him and after a tussle with the wind found him at the north end ready to set up the ladder. He quickly mounted to the edge of the roof when the wind caught under his coat and folded it back over his head. As the hammer and nails were in his pocket and up over his head he was unable to get his hands on them or to pull his coat tails down, so he was compelled to descend again. The next time he put the nails in his mouth and took the hammer in his hand and I followed him up the ladder hanging on to his coat tails. He swatted around a good little while trying to get a few nails in, and I became almost impatient for I had only my common coat on and was getting well soaked. He explained afterward that the wind kept blowing the hammer around so that three licks out of four hit the roof or his fingers instead of the nail. Finally the job was done and we rushed for cover. He took off the overcoat and felt his other coat and found it nice and dry, but after half an hour or so, finding that he was feeling wetter and wetter, he began a second investigation and found the inside of this coat sopping wet, while the outside was nice and dry. He had forgotten when he first felt of his coat, that it, as well as the over coat, were practically inside out while he was working on the roof. The wind and rain continued through the night. . . . In the morning we found the larger part of our floor under water but the kitchen and dining room were all right, the water being merely even with the underside of the floor boards. The front door step was six inches under water. The storm continued through Saturday and Sunday, but by Monday it had reared up so much that it finally fell over on its back and lay quiet.

110

According to Dan Tate this storm broke all records for persistence and has been equalled by few in velocity. Five vessels came ashore between here and Cape Henry, the nearest being visible from the top of our Big Hill. My theory is that a cyclone got becalmed off this coast and could not get away again.

The "wopper flying machine" is coming on all right and will probably be done about Nov. 1st. [October 18, 1903]

The new machine required three weeks for assembling, and the brothers hoped to have the work completed before the first of November. In the meantime, they occasionally practiced with the 1902 glider. In early October, Wilbur wrote to his father about their gliding experiments:

We had two nice days for gliding last week and got in some good practice. We have made a few slight alterations in the machine, causing it to respond to control much more quickly, and enables us to do things with entire safety which before we were uncertain about attempting. We have increased our time for length of flight to 43 seconds which is $1\frac{2}{3}$ our last years record and about three times the best of any one else. We will soon have it up to more than a minute as we are now able to remain practically stationary when a suitable wind blows up a good slope. This is something former experimenters were entirely unable to accomplish. We are very careful and with the increased control and greater experience we encounter less danger than formerly as now we are able to avoid the positions which we formerly had trouble to extricate ourselves from. [October 4, 1903]

Orville recorded the success of October 21st in his diary:

At seven o'clock a wind of 5 meters was blowing at camp from west, which by 8 o'clock had increased to about 6 meters. We took machine soon after to the west slope of Big Hill where we made five glides of about 400 feet. . . . At one o'clock we took machine to north slope of Big Hill, the wind having quite suddenly veered to north with an increase to 7 meters. At top of Big Hill we had 8 meters at first but after 3 or 4 glides wind dropped to $6\frac{1}{2}$ meters, but after a little began increasing again and from 4 o'clock to 5 was blowing about 11 meters at top. Our glides at this time were made from further down the hill, and ran from 30 to 43 seconds. Just before 5 o'clock we returned to the point near top of hill and made 8 or 10 glides, each increasing in time and making new records.

The best flights were as follows, over a course of 400 to 450 feet:

WW	$43\frac{2}{5}$ sec.
OW	$43\frac{3}{4}$ "
OW	45 "
WW	$45\frac{2}{5}$ "
OW	49 "
WW	56 "
OW	$56\frac{3}{5}$ "
OW	1 min. $\frac{1}{2}$ "
WW	59 "

Their work on the new machine progressed slowly into early November, when it was halted by an unexpected problem. As they started the motor for the first time on the machine, a jolt from its back-firing twisted one of the propeller shafts and broke it loose. Both shafts had to be returned to the bicycle shop in Dayton to be strengthened. George Spratt, who had come to camp to witness the tests of the new machine, decided he would not wait out this latest delay, so he took the propeller shafts with him as far as Norfolk and shipped them on to Dayton from there.

Octave Chanute arrived in camp just after Spratt left, but he, too, decided not to wait for the return of the propeller shafts. The weather had turned quite cold and wet, making the long wait especially uncomfortable. Orville described the cold in a letter to Katharine:

About a week ago the weather turned very cold (about zero according to my backbone) and another rain set in which continued for several days without intermittence. We found that a fire was absolutely necessary, especially on account of Spratt, who suffers much from cold. We took one of the carbide cans and, after punching some holes in the bottom for air, built a fire in it inside the building. Of course the smoke was so intense that there was no standing up in the room, so we sat down on the floor about the can with tears streaming down our cheeks enjoying its kindly rays of heat. Everything about the building was sooted up so thoroughly that for several days we couldn't sit down to eat without a whole lot of black soot dropping down in our plates. We decided a change was necessary, so we got a little stove pipe and built a stove out of the can, adding strap iron legs to it, and a number of patent dampers, so that now we have about as good control in our stove as we have on our machine. We are now living in luxurious ease.

Your asking that we telegraph after every storm would soon have us "busted" if complied with. We have been having an almost continuous succession of storms the past few weeks. . . .
[November 1, 1903]

Later that month, Wilbur also commented on the cold in a letter to the family:

The pine we bought of Mr. Baum was hardly worth putting in the stove, it burned up so quickly. We get fourfold value from the live oak. It warms us once to chop it down, second to carry it to camp, third to split it up, and last but not least when we burn it in our patent carbide stove. . . . We are entirely comfortable, and have no trouble keeping warm at nights. In addition to the classifications of last year, to wit, 1, 2, 3 and 4 blanket nights, we now have 5 blanket nights, & 5 blankets & 2 quilts. Next come 5 blankets, 2 quilts & fire; then 5, 2, fire, & hot-water jug. This is as far as we have got so far. Next come the addition of sleeping without undressing, then shoes & hats, and finally overcoats. We intend to be comfortable while we are here. [November 23, 1903]

The waiting time seemed to pass more quickly when they had visitors in camp or when weather permitted glides in the 1902 machine. By mid-November, however, the camp was quiet, and they had to abandon the old machine. Orville explained in a letter to his father and sister:

We are now alone again, the first time for about a month. Mr. Chanute came just as Dr. Spratt left. Spratt, by the way, left about two hours after the breaking of our propeller shafts, taking them along with him to express at Norfolk. We got Pop's letter yesterday saying that they had been received and were nearly ready to be sent back. We will not get them for three or four days yet. At the time they broke we were trying to get the engine in order. The strains on the shafts were enormous as a result of the sprockets being loose. The weight of our machine complete with man will be a little over 700 lbs. . . . Mr. Chanute says that no one before has ever tried to build a machine on such close margins as we have done to our calculations. He said that he nevertheless had more hope of our machine going than any of the others. He seems to think we are pursued by a blind fate from which we are unable to escape. . . . He doesn't seem to think our machines are so much superior as the manner in which we handle them. We are of just the reverse opinion.

The past week and a half has just been a loaf, since we have almost nothing to do on the machine until the shafts come. The weather has been fairly cold at times but with a half cord of wood on hand we have not suffered any. Our carbide can is probably the best stove in Kitty Hawk.

We have had the old machine out only twice in the past three weeks. We took it out day before yesterday to test our starting truck and rails for the new machine. We succeeded in starting five times out of six. As we have no help at present one of us held the machine on the track until the other got on, when he would leave go. The machine of course would coast downhill on the wheels (bicycle hubs running on rails made of 2″ X 4″s) until enough speed was acquired to lift, when the one on board would turn up the rudder and sail off down the hill. We then experimented with one man taking hold of the front rudder (with the other on board) and starting by running a few steps backward till the machine supported. We had no trouble in getting started in this way either, but the fire in the building has so dried out the cloth and wood of the framework of the machine that it is now so rickety as to be unsafe for gliding in high winds. We have now probably made our last glides on it.

As long as we had company there was no chance to write or to do much of anything else. I am now taking up my German and French again, and am making some progress. The lack of a German dictionary prevents me, however, from reading much, the vocabulary in the grammar being quite limited. An article from a German paper, giving some account of our machine, has kept me guessing, as I have only been able to find a few of the words in the vocabulary I have. [November 15, 1903]

November 20—after two weeks of waiting—at last, the repaired propeller shafts arrived from Dayton. Orville later recalled:

We immediately put them in the machine and made another test. A new trouble developed. The sprockets which were screwed on the shafts, and locked with nuts of opposite thread, persisted in coming loose. After many futile attempts to get them fast, we had to give up for that day, and went to bed much discouraged. However, after a night's rest, we got up the next morning in better spirits and resolved to try again.

While in the bicycle business we had become well acquainted with the use of hard tire cement for fastening tires on the rims. We had once used it successfully in repairing a stop watch after several watchsmiths had told us it could not be repaired. If tire cement was good for fastening the hands on a stop watch, why should it not be good for fastening the sprockets on the propeller shaft of a flying machine? We decided to try it. We heated the shafts and sprockets, melted cement into the threads, and screwed them together again. This trouble was over. The sprockets stayed fast. [Orville Wright, "How We Made the First Flight," *Flying and the Aero Club of America Bulletin*, December 1913]

But there was new trouble. Just as the machine was ready for testing, a bad storm caused them to lose another week. They were confined to the building, but they were not idle.

While we were being delayed by the weather we arranged a mechanism to measure automatically the duration of a flight from the time the machine started to move forward to the time it stopped, the distance traveled through the air in that time, and the number of revolutions made by the motor and propeller. A stop watch took the time; an anemometer measured the air traveled through; and a counter took the number of revolutions made by the propellers. The watch, anemometer and revolution counter were all automatically started and stopped simultaneously. From data thus obtained we expected to prove or disprove the accuracy of our calculations. [Orville Wright, "How We Made the First Flight," *Flying and the Aero Club of America Bulletin*, December, 1913]

During this period they also made some indoor tests of the thrust of the propellers, which indicated that they would have ample propulsion for the machine. Wilbur later reported to Chanute, who had been skeptical of their calculations, "We . . . found that we would have plenty of power as the transmission only cost 5 or 10 percent apparently, instead of the thirty percent you had estimated. The thrust of the screw came within three or four pounds of our calculations of what it would do in a fixed position." [December 28, 1903]

Trouble persisted, however. While performing these indoor tests, the Wrights discovered that something else had gone wrong with the propeller shafts: one of the tubular shafts had cracked! This time Orville took the shafts back to Dayton to make new ones, leaving

Wilbur "to keep house alone." They decided to abandon the use of tubes and to replace them with solid steel shafts of a smaller diameter.

Orville was gone two weeks. Five weeks had been lost since the trouble with the propeller shafts first occurred. Eager to try out the machine before the winter weather became any worse, and still hoping to be home for their traditional family Christmas celebration, the brothers "accordingly determined to try the machine at the earliest opportunity instead of waiting for the conditions we desired," as Wilbur reported to Chanute in the December 28, 1903 letter.

By the afternoon of December 12, the day after Orville returned to camp with the new shafts, the machine was again ready. Orville recorded in his diary that day:

Set propeller shafts and got machine outside in afternoon with intention of making a trial. We did not have enough wind for starting from flat and not enough time to go to hill. So we spent some time in running machine along track to see what speed one man could give it. In a 40-ft. run the last 15 feet were covered in $1^{1}/_{2}$ sec. In starting one time the frames supporting the tail were caught on the end of the track and broken. . . .
[Diary D, December 12, 1903]

The next day was Sunday, and the Wrights never broke the Sabbath by working. That was a promise they had long ago made to their father, the bishop. They spent most of the day inside reading—and hoping that weather conditions on the next day would permit them to fly at last.

Monday, December 14, dawned beautiful, but calm. They spent the morning making repairs to the damaged tail of the Flyer. By afternoon the wind was still too light for a start on level ground at the camp, but the brothers decided to make an attempt from the side of Big Kill Devil Hill. They put up a signal to inform members of the Kill Devil lifesaving station—a little over a mile from their camp—that they were ready to make the first trial of the machine. John T. Daniels, Robert Wescott, Thomas Beacham, W. S. Dough, and "Uncle Benny" O'Neal soon joined them to help drag the 750-pound machine over the sand to the big hill, a quarter mile away, and then up the hillside to the selected place.

To make the task a little easier, the brothers had thought of a way to utilize the starting track to maneuver the machine into location. The track was a sixty-foot-long wooden rail made of four fifteen-foot two-by-fours set on edge. The top surface was planed smooth and covered with a thin strip of metal. The Flyer was placed over this track with its sledlike landing skids resting on a truck. The truck consisted of a long plank, the yoke, laid across a smaller plank, to which two small tandem wheels were attached. The wheels were kept on the track by vertical guides. For takeoff, the machine would slide on the wheeled truck, down the length of the monorail, until it had gained enough speed to lift away. To move the Flyer into position on Big Kill Devil Hill that day, the men set the machine on this "Junction Railroad," as the brothers called the monorail, slid the machine along to the end of the track, then picked up a rear section of the track and laid it down again at the front end. This ingenious process must have been tedious, but it enabled the men to move the machine on its wheels nearly the entire way.

Finally they had the Flyer in position. The brothers tossed a coin to see which of them would make the first trial. Wilbur won the toss. In a letter to his family written that evening, he described what happened:

We gave machine first trial today with only partial success. The wind was only about 5 miles an hour so we anticipated difficulty in getting speed enough on our short track (60 ft.) to lift. We took to the hill and after tossing for first whack, which I won, got ready for the start. The wind was a little to one side and the track was not exactly straight downhill which caused the start to be more difficult than it would otherwise have been. However the real trouble was an error in judgment, in turning up too suddenly after leaving the track, and as the machine had barely speed enough for support already, this slowed it down so much that before I could correct the error, the machine began to come down, though turned up at a big angle. Toward the end it began to speed up again but it was too late, and it struck the ground while moving a little to one side, due to wind and a rather bad start. A few sticks in the front rudder were broken, which will take a day or two to repair probably. It was a nice easy landing for the operator. The machinery all worked in entirely satisfactory manner, and seems reliable. The power is ample, and but for a trifling error due to lack of experience with this machine and this method of starting the machine would undoubtedly have flown beautifully. There is now no question of final success. The strength of the machine is all right, the trouble in the front rudder being easily remedied. We anticipate no further trouble in landings. Will probably have made another trial before you receive this unless weather is unfavorable.

[December 14, 1903]

The attempt of December 14 had not been successful, but it was, nevertheless, encouraging. As Orville later recalled:

While the test had shown nothing as to whether the power of the motor was sufficient to keep the machine up, since the landing was made many feet below the starting point, the experiment had demonstrated that the method adopted for launching the machine was a safe and practical one. On the whole, we were much pleased. ["How We Made the First Flight," *Flying and the Aero Club of America Bulletin*, December, 1913]

The brothers were so excited at the partial success that they wanted to let their family know about it even before Wilbur's letter of the fourteenth could reach them. On December 15, still referring to the previous day's attempt, Wilbur sent the following telegram to his father: "MISS JUDGEMENT (sic) AT START REDUCED FLIGHT ONE HUNDRED TWELVE POWER AND CONTROL AMPLE RUDDER ONLY INJURED SUCCESS ASSURED KEEP QUIET."

Repairs to the damaged machine occupied the next couple of days, but on December 17 the Wrights were ready to make another attempt. As Wilbur subsequently explained to Octave Chanute:

Our next flights were on Thursday, December 17th, on which occasion the flights were all made from a level spot about 200 feet west of our buildings. The wind had a velocity of 24 to 27 miles an hour according to the Kitty Hawk anemometer which was almost directly to windward of us, but our measurement made with the English anemometer at a height of 4 ft. from ground was only 20$^{1}/_{2}$ miles. The conditions were very unfavorable as we had a cold gusty north wind blowing almost a gale. Nevertheless as we had set our minds on being home by Christmas, we determined to go ahead. [December 28, 1903]

Orville also recalled the "unfavorable" conditions—the biting cold wind that made preparations difficult, and that caused them to go back indoors frequently to warm their hands over the improvised carbide-can stove. The wind was not only uncomfortable; it was also dangerous, as Orville later admitted. "We thought that by facing the Flyer into a strong wind, there ought to be no trouble in launching it from the level ground about the camp. We realized the difficulties of flying in so high a wind but estimated that the added dangers in flight would be partly compensated for by the slower speed in landing." In retrospect, Orville wondered at their "audacity" in making the attempt that day:

With all the knowledge and skill acquired in thousands of flights in the last ten years, I would hardly think today of making my first flight in a strange machine in a twenty-seven-mile wind, even if I knew that the machine had already been flown and was safe. After these years of experience I look with amazement upon our audacity in attempting flights with a new and untried machine under such circumstances. Yet faith in our calculations and the design of this first machine, based upon our tables of air pressures, secured by months of careful laboratory work, and confidence in our system of control developed by three years of actual experience in balancing gliders in the air had convinced us that the machine was capable of lifting and maintaining itself in the air, and that, with a little practice, it could be safely flown. ["How We Made the First Flight," _Flying and the Aero Club of America Bulletin_, December, 1913]

Their signal to the Kill Devil life saving station for assistance brought members J. T. Daniels, W. S. Dough, and A. D. Etheridge, as well as W. C. Brinkley of Manteo; and Johnny Moore, a boy from Nags Head, to witness the historic event that was about to occur. Wilbur had used his first turn for the unsuccessful trial of December 14, so it was now Orville's turn to take the controls of the machine. But first Orville positioned his camera, a Korona, on its tripod and prepared it to record the takeoff. He instructed J. T. Daniels to snap the camera just as the Flyer left the track. Daniels's timing was perfect; the result is a priceless image of the epochal instant in history when man achieved powered flight.

The machine started very slowly in the face of the high wind, and Wilbur was able to stay alongside to balance it until it lifted from the track after a forty-foot run. He had just let go of the wing when Daniels took the picture.

In the air, Orville had difficulty controlling the machine, partly because of the gusting winds and partly because of his inexperience with this machine. With a sudden dart, the Flyer hit the ground, just a little over 120 feet from the point at which it had lifted into the air. Despite the abrupt end to his flight, Orville was pleased. As he recalled later, "This flight lasted only 12 seconds, but it was nevertheless the first in the history of the world in which a machine carrying a man had raised itself by its own power into the air in full flight, had sailed forward without reduction of speed, and had finally landed at a point as high as that from which it started" ("How We Made the First Flight").

Three other flights were made that day, with Orville and Wilbur taking turns at the controls. The last trial was the longest, covering a ground distance of 852 feet in fifty-nine seconds. More flights would have been attempted, but a sudden gust of wind intervened, as Orville later described:

While we were standing about discussing this last flight, a sudden strong gust of wind struck the machine and began to turn it over. Everybody made a rush for it. Wilbur, who was at one end, seized the front, Mr. Daniels and I, who were behind, tried to stop it by holding to the rear uprights. All our efforts were vain. The machine rolled over and over. Daniels, who had retained his grip, was carried along with it, and was thrown about head over heels inside of the machine. Fortunately he was not seriously injured, though badly bruised in falling about against the motor, chain guides, etc. The ribs in the surfaces of the machine were broken, the motor injured and the chain guides badly bent, so that all possibility of further flights with it for that year were at an end. ["How We Made the First Flight," *Flying and the Aero Club of America Bulletin*, December, 1913]

Elated by the success they had had that day. the brothers walked the four miles to the weather station at Kitty Hawk to send a telegram to their father, announcing the news.

The Wrights knew that the day's events were only the beginning of what had to be accomplished before manned flight would be practical. After all, their longest flight of the day had lasted less than a minute. Nevertheless, those who understood the significance of the events of December 17 would share the brothers' satisfaction. Few would know better what the Wrights had accomplished than their colleague Octave Chanute. In reporting their success to Chanute, Wilbur wrote:

The "Junction Railroad" worked perfectly and a good start was obtained every time. The machine would run along the track about 40 ft. propelled by the screws alone, as we did not feel it safe to have strangers touch the machine. It would then rise and fly directly against the wind at a speed of about 10 miles an hour. The first flight was of about 12 seconds' duration and the last 59 seconds. The controling mechanisms operated more powerfully than in our old machine so that we nearly always

turned the rudders more than was really necessary and thus kept up a somewhat undulating course especially in the first flights. Under the prevailing conditions we did not feel it safe to rise far from the ground and this was the cause of our flights being no longer than they were, for we did not have sufficient room to maneuver in such a gusty gale. Consequently we were frequently on the point of touching the ground and once scratched it deeply but rose again and continued the flight. Those who understand the real significance of the conditions under which we worked will be surprised rather at the length than the shortness of the flights made with an unfamiliar machine after less than one minute's practice. The machine possesses greater capacity of being controled than any of our former machines.

One of the most gratifying features of the trials was the fact that all our calculations were shown to have worked out with absolute exactness so far as we can see, though we have not yet made our final computations on the performance of the machine. [December 28, 1903]

Wilbur and Orville arrived back home in Dayton on December 23, in time for Christmas as promised. Already the news was out, and reporters were hounding the family for details. Bishop Wright and Katharine had no more information about the flights than the brief telegram. They, too, were eagerly awaiting the return of the boys for more news. The Bishop did, however, make this statement about his sons: "Wilbur is 36, Orville 32, and they are as inseparable as twins. For several years they have read up on aeronautics as a physician would read his books, and they have studied, discussed, and experimented together. Natural workmen, they have invented, constructed, and operated their gliders, and finally their 'Wright Flyer,' jointly, all at their personal expense. About equal credit is due each" (Bishop Milton Wright to Carl Dienstbach, December 22, 1903).

When they were ready, Wilbur and Orville made their statement to the press. After describing the trials of December 17 and attempting to correct misinformation which had already been printed in the newspapers, the brothers concluded their statement as follows:

Only those who are acquainted with practical aeronautics can appreciate the difficulties of attempting the first trials of a flying machine in a 25 mile gale. As winter was already well set in, we should have postponed our trials to a more favorable season, but for the fact that we were determined, before returning home, to know whether the machine possessed sufficient power to fly, sufficient strength to withstand the shock of landings, and sufficient capacity of control to make flight safe in boisterous winds, as well as in calm air. When these points had been definitely established, we at once packed our goods and returned home, knowing that the age of the flying machine had come at last. [Statement by the Wright brothers to the Associated Press, January 5, 1904]

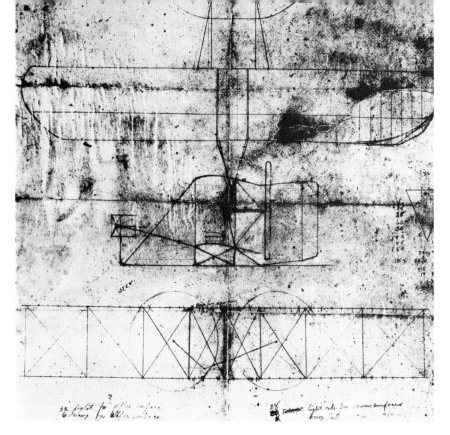

A three-view sketch of the Wrights' 1903 machine with notations in Wilbur's handwriting. This preliminary sketch was originally drawn in pencil on brown wrapping paper.

Franklin Institute Science Museum, Philadelphia, Pa.

The camp in 1903, showing the new building added that year.

We are expecting the most interesting results of any of our seasons of experiment. . . . We were delayed a week by the nonarrival of some of our goods, but now have everything. The upper surface of new machine is completed. It is far ahead of anything we have built before. The lower surface is about half done. It will probably be nearly Nov. 1st before we are ready for trial, especially if we have some nice soaring weather.
[Wilbur Wright to Octave Chanute, October 16, 1903]

Orville assembling the 1903 machine in the new camp building.

The 1903 machine in front of the camp buildings, with Wilbur standing in the doorway.

The early part of the glides were practically soaring, our speed over ground being from one to two feet per second, often for distances of 25 to 75 feet. We took a number of measurements of the relative wind by running along by side of machine with the anemometer. . . . Many of these flights were at heights from 40 to 60 feet, by far the highest gliding we have ever done. We made 3 pictures.

[Orville Wright's Diary D, October 21, 1903]

This 1903 photograph of a glide on the 1902 machine is one of the pictures mentioned in Orville's diary for October 21. The camp buildings are visible in the distance.

Rain and wind continued through entire night, forming ponds all about camp. Temperature lower. Air so damp and cold that we made a stove out of a carbide can and built small fire, avoiding smoke as much as possible by sitting on floor. Inclosed small space with carpets, etc., to keep out wind. [Orville Wright's Diary D, October 25, 1903]

The Wrights' "living room" at camp in 1903, showing carbide-can stove and rugs hung to prevent drafts.

After many attempts to fasten sprockets we finally succeeded by filling thread with tire cement. The engine ran very irregularly, jerking the chains, and shaking the machine terribly. We discovered the trouble lay in the gasoline feed, and, after fixing valve so that the vibration could not change it, we had no further trouble from that source. . . . After dinner we arranged to measure the thrust by supporting center skids on rollers and fastening one end of machine, while we attached a rope to the other end, which ran over a pulley and carried a 50 lb. box of sand. Besides lifting the sand we got an additional pull of 16 to 18 lbs. on the scales, which made the total thrust of the screws 132 and 136 lbs. at a speed of 350 revolutions per min. Our confidence in the success of the machine is now greater than ever before. [Orville Wright's Diary D, November 21, 1903]

The motor of the 1903 Flyer as exhibited in 1928 with the reconstructed machine.

*Orville standing beside the
1903 Flyer.*

A front view of the 1903 machine.

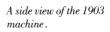

A side view of the 1903 machine.

Library of Congress

Our track for starting the machine (total cost about $4.00) amused Mr. Chanute considerably, as Langley is said to have spent nearly $50,000.00 on his starting device which failed in the end to give a proper start, he claims. At least this is the reason he gives for the failure last month. We have only tried ours with the little machine, so far, but it seems to work well. [Wilbur Wright to his father and sister, November 23, 1903]

The launching technique devised by the Wrights involved a sixty-foot sectioned rail (nicknamed by them "Junction Railroad.") The skids of the machine were laid on a truck that could run freely along the rail on two small tandem wheels. The machine was restrained until the engine was ready, and then released, sliding down the rail until it gained sufficient speed to lift up from the truck and fly.

At the turn of the century, lifesaving stations were located at seven-mile intervals all along the coast of North Carolina. During their stay on the Outer Banks, the Wrights were friendly with the men of the stations both at Kitty Hawk and at Kill Devil Hills. The Kill Devil Hills station, shown here, was located a little over a mile from the Wrights' camp. Soon after arriving at camp in 1903, Orville wrote to his sister Katharine, "Have Lorin mount four or five of those pictures of the Life Saving Station," so that he could give them to the men.

The Wrights arranged to signal the crew of the Kill Devil Hills station when they were ready to attempt a powered flight. They needed the men both as witnesses and as assistants to maneuver the heavy machine on the ground.

132

We spent morning in making repairs on tail, and truck for starting. At half past one o'clock we put out signal for station men, and started for hill, which took us about 40 minutes. After testing engine, with help of men (Bob Wescott, John T. Daniels, Tom Beacham, W. S. Dough, and Uncle Benny O'Neal), we took machine 150 ft. uphill and laid track on 8°50' slope. A couple small boys, who had come with the men from the station, made a hurried departure over the hill for home on hearing the engine start. We tossed up coin to decide who should make first trial, and Will won. After getting adjustments of engine ready I took right end of machine. Will got on. When all was ready Will attempted to release fastening to rail, but the pressure due to weight of machine and thrust of screws was so great that he could not get it loose. We had to get a couple of the men to help push machine back till rope was slipped loose. While I was signaling man at other end to leave go, but before I myself was ready, Will started machine. I grabbed the upright the best I could and off we went. By the time we had reached the last quarter of the third rail (about 35 to 40 feet) the speed was so great I could stay with it no longer. I snapped watch as machine passed end of track. (It had raised from track six or eight feet from end.) The machine turned up in front and rose to a height of about 15 feet from ground at a point somewhat in neighborhood of 60 feet from end of track. After thus losing most of its headway it gradually sank to ground turned up at an angle of probably 20° incidence. The left wing was lower than the right so that in landing it struck first. The machine swung around and scraped the front skids (bows running out to front rudder) so deep in sand that one was broken, and twisted around until the main strut and brace were also broken, besides the rear spar to lower surface of front rudder. Will forgot to shut off engine for some time, so that the record of screw turns was mostly taken while the machine was on the ground. The engine made 602 rev. in 35$\frac{1}{2}$ s. Time of flight from end of track was 3$\frac{1}{2}$ sec. for a distance of 105 ft. Angle of descent for the 105 feet was 4°55'. Speed of wind was between 4 and 8 miles. [Orville Wright's Diary D, December 14, 1903]

The 1903 Flyer on the track on Big Kill Devil Hill just prior to the unsuccessful trial of December 14. Also shown are the four men from the lifesaving station and the two small boys mentioned in Orville's diary entry for that day.

The end of the unsuccessful trial of December 14, with Wilbur in the damaged machine.

Library of Congress

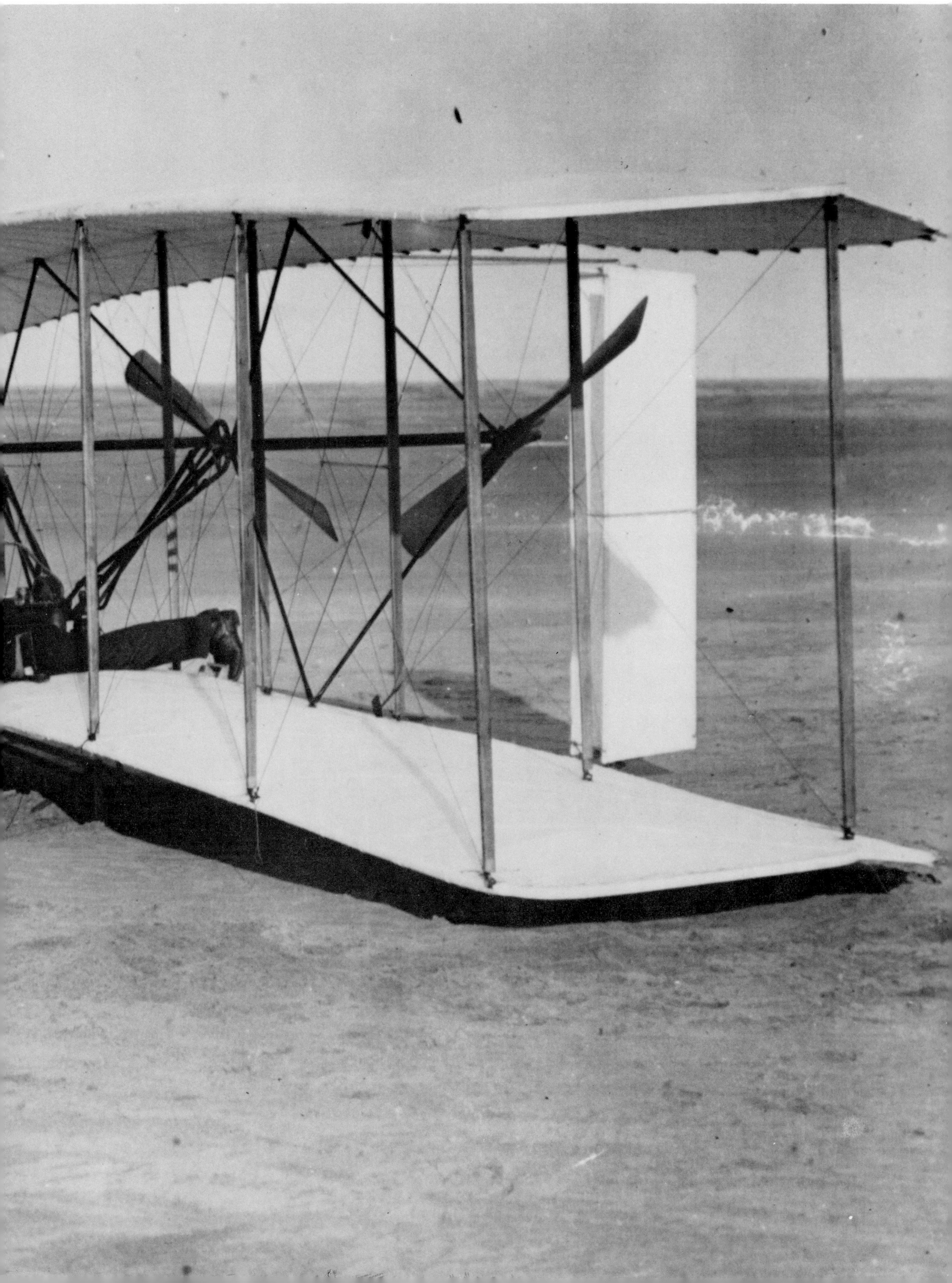

When we got up a wind of between 20 and 25 miles was blowing from the north. We got the machine out early and put out the signal for the men at the station. Before we were quite ready, John T. Daniels, W. S. Dough, A. D. Etheridge, W. C. Brinkley of Manteo, and Johnny Moore of Nags Head arrived. After running the engine and propellers a few minutes to get them in working order, I got on the machine at 10:35 for the first trial. The wind, according to our anemometers at this time, was blowing a little over 20 miles (corrected) 27 miles according to the Government anemometer at Kitty Hawk. On slipping the rope the machine started off increasing in speed to probably 7 or 8 miles. The machine lifted from the truck just as it was entering on the fourth rail. Mr. Daniels took a picture just as it left the tracks. I found the control of the front rudder quite diffi-cult on account of its being balanced too near the center and thus had a tendency to turn itself when started so that the rudder was turned too far on one side and then too far on the other. As a result the machine would rise suddenly to about 10 ft. and then as suddenly, on turning the rud-der, dart for the ground. A sudden dart when out about 100 feet from the end of the tracks ended the flight. Time about 12 seconds (not known exactly as watch was not promptly stopped). The lever for throwing off the engine was broken, and the skid under the rudder cracked. . . . After repairs, at 20 min. after 11 o'clock Will made the second trial. The course was about like mine, up and down but a little longer over the ground though about the same in time. Dist. not measured but about 175 ft. Wind speed not quite so strong. With the aid of the station men present, we picked the machine up and carried it back to the starting ways. At about 20 minutes till 12 o'clock I made the third trial. When out about the same distance as Will's, I met with a strong gust from the left which raised the left wing and sidled the machine off to the right in a lively manner. I immediately turned the rudder to bring the machine down and then worked the end control. Much to our surprise, on reach-ing the ground the left wing struck first, showing the lateral control of this machine much more effective than on any of our former ones. At the time of its sidling it had raised to a height of probably 12 to 14 feet. At just 12 o'clock Will started on the fourth and last trip. The machine started off with its ups and downs as it had before, but by the time he had gone over three or four hundred feet he had it under much better control, and was traveling on a fairly even course. It proceeded in this manner till it reached a small hummock out about 800 feet from the starting ways, when it began its pitching again and suddenly darted into the ground. The front rudder frame was badly broken up, but the main frame suffered none at all. The distance over the ground was 852 feet in 59 seconds. The engine turns was 1071, but this included several seconds while on the starting ways and probably about a half second after landing. The jar of landing had set the watch on machine back so that we have no exact record for the 1071 turns. Will took a picture of my third flight just before the gust struck the machine. The machine left the ways success-fully at every trial, and the tail was never caught by the truck as we had feared.

After removing the front rudder, we carried the machine back to camp. We set the machine down a few feet west of the building, and while standing about discussing the last flight, a sudden gust of wind struck the machine and started to turn it over. All rushed to stop it. Will who was near one end ran to the front, but too late to do any good. Mr. Daniels and myself seized spars at the rear, but to no purpose. The machine gradually turned over on us. Mr. Daniels, having had no experience in handling a machine of this kind, hung on to it from the inside, and as a result was knocked down and turned over and over with it as it went. His escape was miraculous, as he was in with the engine and chains. The engine legs were all broken off, the chain guides badly bent, a number of uprights, and nearly all the rear ends of the ribs were broken. One spar only was broken.

  After dinner we went to Kitty Hawk to send off telegram to M. W. (Bishop Milton Wright, their father). While there we called on Capt. and Mrs. Hobbs, Dr. Cogswell and the station men.

[Orville Wright's Diary D, December 17, 1903]

Form No. 168.

THE WESTERN UNION TELEGRAPH COMPANY.

INCORPORATED
23,000 OFFICES IN AMERICA. CABLE SERVICE TO ALL THE WORLD.

RECEIVED at

176 C KA CS 33 Paid. Via Norfolk Va

Kitty Hawk N C Dec 17

Bishop M Wright

   7 Hawthorne St

Success four flights thursday morning all against twenty one mile

wind started from Level with engine power alone average speed

through air thirty one miles longest 57 seconds inform Press

home ~~####~~ Christmas .   Orevelle Wright 525P

Library of Congress

137

The historic message was sent from the Kitty Hawk weather station to the weather station at Norfolk, Virginia, and then relayed by telephone to a commercial telegraph office. Two errors were made in the transmission: fifty-nine seconds became fifty-seven seconds, and Orville's name was misspelled.

Orville set his camera on a tripod and adjusted the lens so that a point a few feet from the end of the starting rail would fall on the center of the five-by-seven-inch glass plate. He asked John T. Daniels of the Kill Devil lifesaving station to snap the picture when the Flyer passed that point. The result was this remarkable photograph of the Flyer just as it lifted into the air.

Library of Congress

The third flight of the 17th,
Orville again at the controls.
(No photograph was taken of
the second flight, which
Wilbur made.)

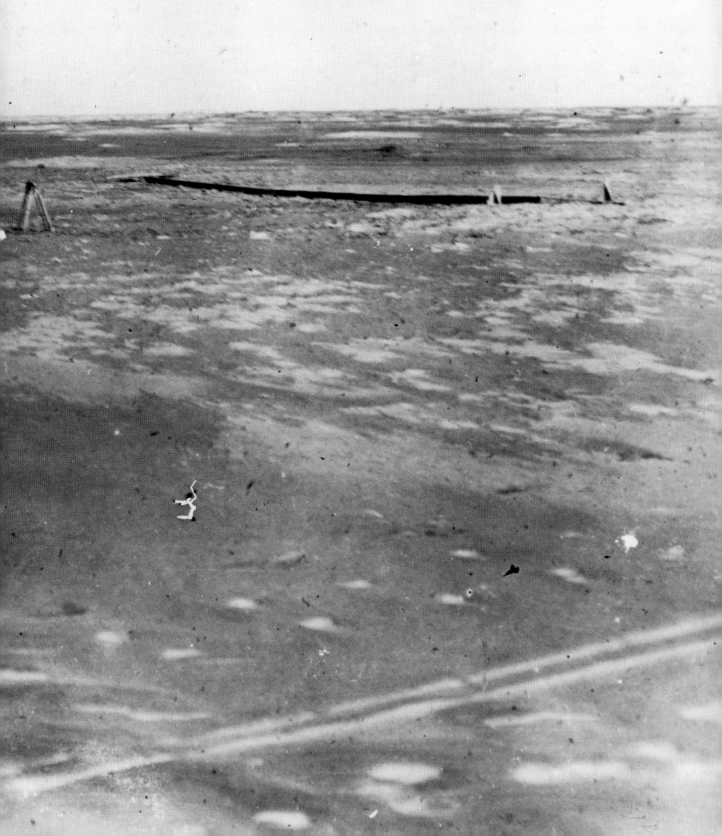

144

This photograph of the 1903 machine was made at the end of its last flight, shortly before a gust of wind over-turned the machine and brought the tests to an end for that season.

Library of Congress

52

by noon and got the
machine out on the
tracks in front of the
building ready for a
trial from the level.
The wind was gradually
dying and by the time
we were ready was blow-
ing only about 4 to 5
meters per. sec. After
waiting several hours
to see whether it would
breeze up again we took
the machine in.

Thursday, Dec. 17th

When we got up a
wind of between 20 and
25 miles was blowing from
the north. We got the
machine out early and
put out the signal for the
men at the station. Before
we were quite ready, John
T. Daniels, W. S. Dough,
A. D. Etheridge, W. C.
Brinkley of Manteo, and
Johnny Moore, of Nags
Head arrived. After

53

running the engine and
propellers a few min-
utes to get them in working
order, I got on the machine
at 10:35 for the first
trial. The wind according
to our anemometers at
this time was blowing a
little over 20 miles (corrected) 27 miles accord-
ing to the Government an-
emometer at Kitty Hawk.
On slipping the rope
the machine started off
increasing in speed to
probably 7 or 8 miles. The
machine lifted from the
truck just as it was
entering on the fourth rail.
Mr. Daniels took a pic-
ture just as it left the
tracks. I found the
control of the front rud-
der quite difficult on
account of its being bal-
anced too near the center
and thus had a tendency
to turn itself when started
so that the rudder was
turned too far on one
side and then too

145

A portion of Orville Wright's diary entry for the historic flights of December 17, 1903, in his own handwriting.

1904
1905

. . . after several seasons we found ourselves standing at a fork in the road.

[Wilbur Wright to Albert F. Zahm, December 22, 1905]

As important as the 1903 flights were, they merely showed the potential of the Wrights' powered Flyer. Wilbur and Orville began almost immediately to construct an even sturdier machine to hold a more powerful engine. They decided to look for a practice area closer to home in order to spend more time testing their machines. So for the next few years they did not go back to their camp in North Carolina.

They obtained permission to use a field, owned by Torrence Huffman, located about eight miles from Dayton. Known both as Huffman Prairie and Simms Station (the latter for the nearest interurban trolley stop on the Dayton-Springfield line), the field served as the Wrights' practice area for the two new planes they developed in 1904 and 1905.

Although the local field was convenient, it did not suit the Wrights as well as the area at Kitty Hawk. When Octave Chanute commented, "I rather suspect that your experimental ground is not as favorable as that at Kitty Hawk," Wilbur responded:

You are quite right in thinking our Kitty Hawk grounds possess advantages not found at our present location, but we must learn to accommodate ourselves to circumstances. At Kitty Hawk we had unlimited space and wind enough to make starting easy with a short track. If the wind was very light we could utilize the hills if necessary in getting the initial velocity. Here we must depend on a long track, and light winds or even dead calms. We are in a large meadow of about 100 acres. It is skirted on the west and north by trees. This not only shuts off the wind somewhat but also probably gives a slight down trend. However, this matter we do not consider any thing serious. The greater troubles are the facts that in addition to cattle there have been a dozen or more horses in the pasture and as it is surrounded by barb wire fencing we have been at much trouble to get them safely away before making trials. Also the ground is an old swamp and is filled with grassy hummocks some six inches high so that it resembles a prairie-dog town. This makes the track laying slow work. While we are getting ready the favorable opportunities slip away, and we are usually up against a rain storm, a dead calm, or a wind blowing at right angles to the track. Today we had our first decent chance, but as the margin was very small, we were not skillful enough to really get started. The first two flights were for a distance of a little more than a hundred feet, and the third two hundred and twenty five feet. On this one Orville almost got away, but after about 200 ft. he allowed the machine to turn up a little too much and it stalled it. He had a speed of about 18 miles on leaving the track, but the rise necessary to gain a little room for maneuvering reduced this to about 16 miles, and as the wind was blowing only 8 miles and unsteady at that, the resistance was too high to permit rapid acceleration,

148

owing to the great angle of incidence required. To get started under such conditions requires perfect management. We are a little rusty. With a little more track and a little more practice we hope to get a real start before long and then we will see what the machine can really do in the way of flying. The machine landed nicely each time without any injury at all. [June 21, 1904]

The sixty-foot starting track was long enough for launching a machine in the winds at Kitty Hawk, but not in the lighter winds over Huffman Prairie. The Wrights had trouble finding an area of the pasture smooth enough for the longer rail that was needed. The difficulties of starting the 1904 Flyer continued to frustrate the brothers until they hit upon an idea for a new launching device. In September 1904, they began using a weight-and-derrick system to give the Flyer enough acceleration for lift-off. A sixteen-hundred-pound weight was pulled to the top of a derrick and attached to the Flyer by ropes and pulleys. When the weight dropped, it catapulted the machine along the track and into the air. With the help of this device, the Wrights made 105 flights in 1904, their longest one being five minutes and eight seconds, over a three-mile distance.

During the 1904 tests, the brothers learned to fly in a circle.

When we had familiarized ourselves with the operation of the machine in more or less straight flights, we decided to try a complete circle. At first we did not know just how much movement to give in order to make a circle of a given size. On the first three trials we found that we had started a circle on too large a radius to keep within the boundaries of the small field in which we were operating. Accordingly, a landing was made each time, without accident, merely to avoid passing beyond the boundaries of the field. On the fourth trial, made on the 20th of September, a complete circle was made, and the machine was brought safely to rest after having passed the starting point. Thereafter we repeatedly made circles, and on the 9th of November made four circles of the field in a flight lasting a few seconds over five minutes. [Wilbur Wright, "Summary of Experiments of 1904," court deposition, February 1912]

In May 1905, the brothers began to assemble a new machine, a process meticulously recorded by Wilbur:

Began setting up machine at Simms. The 1905 machine is very similar to 1904 but the curvature of ribs is 1/20 while that of 1904 is about 1/25 to 1/30 at end of season. The two surfaces with uprights, wires, skids, &c., weighed 252 lbs. With engine, & transmission and everything complete except rudder & tail 590 lbs. Tail 10 lbs. F[ront] rudder & frame 64 lbs. Water 30 lbs. Gasoline 6 lbs. Man 145 lbs. Total 845 lbs. A few things not weighed. [Diary F, May 23, 1905]

They again made their trials at Huffman Prairie, modifying the machine and their handling as needed to improve the Flyer's performance. Wilbur later recalled the experiments of that year:

In 1905 we built another machine and resumed our experiments in the same field near Dayton, Ohio. . . . During all the flights we had made up to this time we had kept close to the ground, in order that, in case we met any new and mysterious phenomenon, we could make a safe landing. With only one life to spend we did not consider it advisable to attempt to explore mysteries at such great height from the ground that a fall would put an end to our investigations and leave the mystery unsolved.

["Summary of Experiments of 1904"]

Toward the end of 1905, Wilbur confidently wrote: "Our 1905 improvements have given such results as to justify the assertion that flying has been transferred from the realm of scientific problems to that of useful arts." Although most the construction changes were not apparent to the eye, the Wrights improved the engine, propellers, controls, and overall structural strength of their machine. The reliability and endurance of their flights increased as the brothers continued their tests. On the forty-sixth flight of the season, Wilbur stayed airborne for thirty-eight minutes and three seconds, making about thirty rounds of the field—over twenty-four miles! The 1905 Flyer was the world's first practical airplane. Not only could it stay in the air for more than a few minutes, but it could also bank, turn, and do a figure eight. The brothers were confident that they "were ready to place flying machines on the market."

Earlier that year the Wrights had written to their congressman, offering to develop a practical Flyer for the United States Government. The letter summarized their achievements of the previous season.

The series of aeronautical experiments upon which we have been engaged for the past five years has ended in the production of a flying-machine of the type fitted for practical use. It not only flies through the air at high speed, but it also lands without being wrecked. During the year 1904 one hundred and five flights were made at our experimenting station, on the Huffman prairie, east of the city; and though our experience in handling the machine has been too short to give any high degree of skill, we nevertheless succeeded, toward the end of the season, in making two flights of five minutes each in which we sailed round and round the field until a distance of about three miles had been covered, at a speed of thirty-five miles an hour . . . .

The numerous flights in straight lines, in circles, and over "S"-shaped courses, in calms and in winds, have made it quite certain that flying has been brought to a point where it can be made of great practical use in various ways, one of which is that of scouting and carrying messages in time of war. . . .

If you can find it convenient to ascertain whether this is a subject of interest to our own government, it would oblige us greatly, as early information on this point will aid us in making our own plans for the future. . . . [Wilbur Wright to Hon. Robert Nevin, January 18, 1905]

The United States Government was slow to pick up on the idea, however, and by the end of 1905 the Wrights decided to look elsewhere for a buyer. In November Wilbur wrote to the French ambassador:

About two years ago we succeeded in making the first free flight through the air with a motor-driven aeroplane. Since that time we have been busily engaged in developing the invention to the point of practicability. Though the difficulty of the task was increased not a little by the necessity of avoiding the eyes of the curious during the necessary preliminary flights we have finally carried the machine through the experimental stage and are now ready to offer it for sale as a secret practical invention.

We are about to make a formal proposition to the French war office, but we realize that it will seem incredible not only that long flights have really been made with motor aeroplanes, but also that they have been made so quietly as to escape the attention of the newspapers. We suggest, therefore, that you send an attaché to Dayton at once to make such careful preliminary investigation on the spot as will enable the war office to judge whether the offer is worthy of serious consideration. [Wilbur Wright to J.-J. Jusserand, November 28, 1905]

The Wright brothers had not expected to profit financially in the early years of experiments; the distinction of being the first men to fly seemed reward enough for their personal effort and expense. Now, however, as they considered the practical uses of the Flyer, they approached further development of the machine with an eye toward recouping something for their investment. As Wilbur explained in a letter at the close of 1905:

151

When my brother and I began experimenting in 1900 it was purely for the pleasure of it. We did not expect to get back a cent of the money we spent. Consequently we agreed with each other that it should under no circumstances be permitted to infringe upon the time and money needed for our business.

The results of the experiments were made public promptly for the encouragement of others. But after several seasons we found ourselves standing at a fork in the road. On the one hand we could continue playing with the problem of flying so long as youth and leisure would permit but carefully avoiding those features which would require continuous effort and the expenditure of considerable sums of money. On the other hand we believed that if we would take the risk of devoting our entire time and financial resources we could conquer the difficulties in the path to success before increasing years impaired our physical activity. We finally decided to make the attempt but as our financial future was at stake were compelled to regard it as a strict business proposition until such time as we had recouped ourselves. From first to last our experiments have been conducted entirely at our own expense, and up to the present not one cent of financial return has been received. We shall endeavor to secure our pay in such a way as will permit the world in general to receive the benefit of the invention within a

reasonably short time, with the least possible restriction on progress. It would interfere with our plans if we should make public at once a description of our machine and methods.

[Wilbur Wright to Albert F. Zahm, December 22, 1905]

Convincing people that flight was not only possible but actually practical, too, was harder than the Wrights had expected. Once the initial excitement of the First Flight had passed, people generally paid little attention to the work of the Wrights for the next few years. A notable exception, however, was Amos Root, publisher of a magazine entitled *Gleanings in Bee Culture*. Root had witnessed one of the 1904 trials at Huffman Prairie and had seen Wilbur make the first circular flight in a powered machine. With more vision than most of his contemporaries, Root concluded his published account of the event, stating:

When Columbus discovered America he did not know what the outcome would be, and no one at that time knew; and I doubt if the wildest enthusiast caught a glimpse of what really did come from his discovery. In a like manner these two brothers have probably not even a faint glimpse of what their discovery is going to bring to the children of men. No one living can give a guess along this line, much better than any one living could conjecture the final outcome of Columbus' experiment when he pushed off through the trackless waters. Possibly we may be able to fly *over* the north pole, even if we should *not* succeed in tracking the "stars and stripes" to its uppermost end.

152

[Amos I. Root, *Gleanings in Bee Culture*, January 1, 1905]

We are about ready to commence setting up our new machine. We have arranged for an experimental station about eight miles east of Dayton and so will not go to Kitty Hawk this Spring. [Wilbur Wright to Octave Chanute, March 29, 1904]

The Wrights' second powered machine, shown at Huffman Prairie, May 1904, with Orville (left) and Wilbur.

153

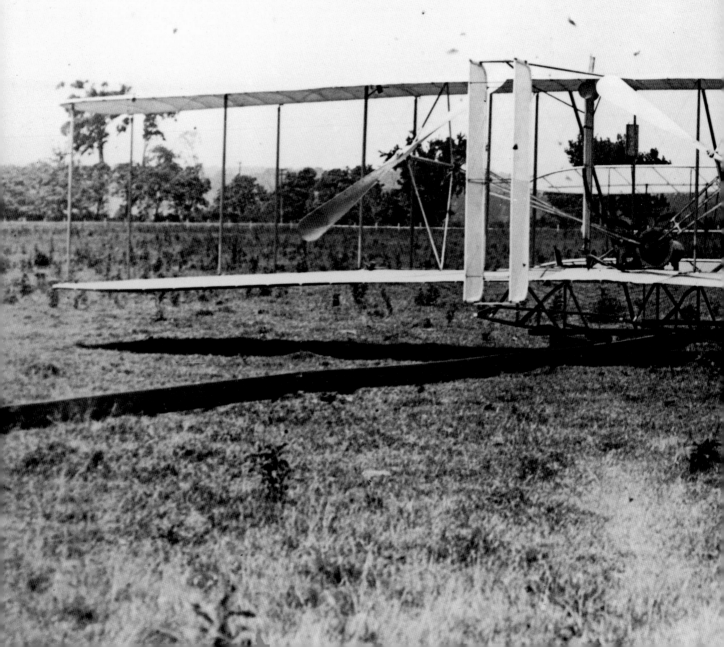

The 1904 machine on the starting track at Huffman Prairie. The "Junction Railroad" was less effective on the rough ground of this practice area than when used at Kill Devil Hills, and the Wrights eventually had to devise a new system for starting.

Flight over practice area at Huffman Prairie in the 1904 Flyer.

Library of Congress

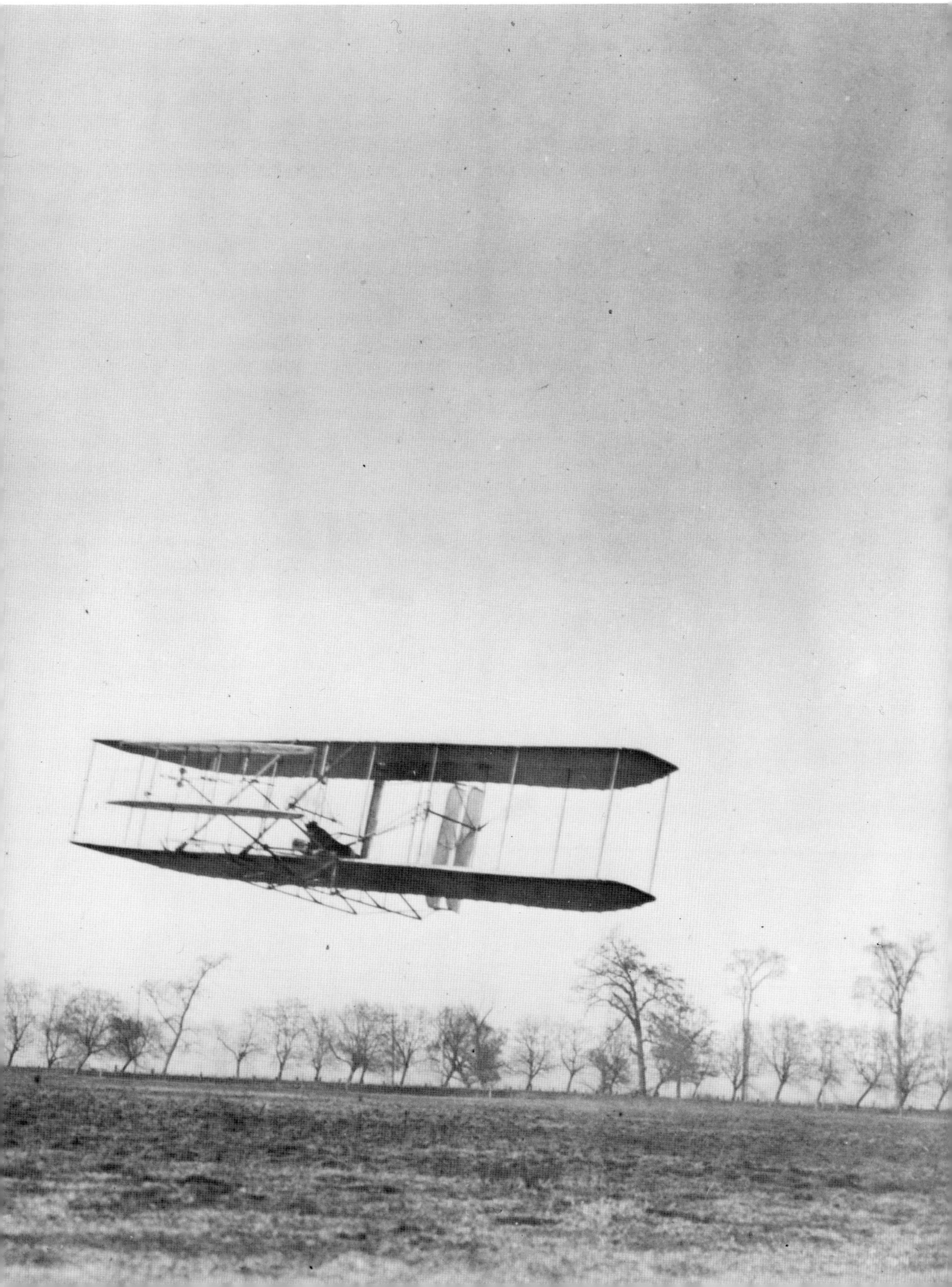

Our chief objection to the Huffman Prairie grounds is not the lack of seclusion but the lack of room. We need a place where we can start at the building and fly in any direction. [Wilbur Wright to Octave Chanute, March 26, 1905]

158

This photo of the first trial for the 1905 season, made on June 23, shows the catapult launching device (at right) devised by the Wrights to compensate for the poor starting conditions at the Simms Station field.

Library of Congress

Orville Wright on a 12-mile flight over Huffman Prairie, September 29, 1905.

Our experiments have been progressing quite satisfactorily, and we are rapidly acquiring skill in the new methods of operating the machine. We may soon attempt trips beyond the confines of the field. [Wilbur Wright to Octave Chanute, September 17, 1905]

1908

I am on my way to Kitty Hawk to get a camp in shape for a little practice before undertaking the official trials at Washington and in France. . . .

[Wilbur Wright to Octave Chanute, April 8, 1908]

For a period of two and a half years, the Wrights quietly engaged in making improvements on their Flyer and conducting negotiations with possible clients. The brothers felt that secrecy was important during this time so that no one could steal their invention before their own rights were secure. They had not flown since October 1905.

Just when it seemed as if the negotiations were in vain, their luck turned. In February 1908, the Wrights received a contract from the U.S. Army Signal Corps. Six weeks later, they also had a contract with a wealthy Frenchman who intended to form a syndicate to buy the rights to manufacture, sell, or license the use of the Wright machine in France.

Now the pressure was on. The Wrights had not one, but two contracts, each based on a successful demonstration of their machine. The Signal Corps required a machine "capable of carrying two men and sufficient fuel supplies for a flight of 125 miles, with a speed of at least 40 miles an hour." Both the pilot and the passenger were to be in a sitting position, not lying prone as the operator had had to be in the previous Wright machines. So the brothers had to design a new control system. They promised delivery in two hundred days for $25,000.

Wilbur outlined the terms of the French contract in a letter to Octave Chanute:

I am not sure that I mentioned the fact that we have been in negotiation for the sale of our French rights for several months past, and that we finally accepted the offer of M. Lazare Weiler who is the head of many large enterprises in France. The contract was closed on the basis of 500,000 frs. cash and one half the founders' shares, the founders' shares being entitled to one half the profits, after interest has been paid on the cash capital. We are to make two flights, each of 50 kilometers within an hour. The flight in each case must be made within four days of the time we may designate for the first attempt, and must be not later than five months from the first of June. In case of high wind or breakage of machine the time required for return of flying conditions is omitted in counting the four days.

We would have preferred to leave the arrangement of European sales rest till after the U.S. business had been finished, but when it came to accepting or refusing a direct offer, we thought on the whole, it would be safer to accept it. It includes both government & commercial rights for France & its colonies. The contract also provides for the sale of four additional machines beyond that used in the demonstrations; we are to have an extra 20,000 frs. each for these machines, 80,000 frs. in all. About half will be profit. We are a little worried for fear one of us will have to go to France before the U.S. work is finished. [April 8, 1908]

There was no time to waste. The Wrights would have to work on fulfillment of both contracts simultaneously. Furthermore, they would have to regain their skills in piloting, since neither brother had flown for close to three years. They decided to return to their old camp at Kill Devil Hills, where they could count on better winds and more space and privacy for the intense period of practice they needed.

Wilbur set out ahead to prepare the camp. He arrived at Kitty Hawk on April 9, followed a week later by Charles Furnas, a mechanic from Dayton. Orville arrived on April 25. It was the brothers' first trip back to camp since the historic flights of December 1903.

In their absence, storms had ravaged the campsite. Wilbur surveyed the damage and wrote to Orville:

I reached K.H. last evening about 7 o'clock. . . . This morning I went down to camp . . . and found everything in ruins. The side walls and rafters of the old building are still standing but the paper and sheeting are off the roof and the north door is gone. The floor is several feet underground. The new building is clear down. The worst feature of the situation is the lack of any place to live while putting up the new building. . . . It will be a big job getting the lumber down to the old neighborhood. The best place except for mosquitoes would be near the old fish landing but the bugs that bite would probably eat us up before we fairly got to experimenting so I think now that I will go down near the old place again. I have arranged for a couple of men to help put up the building as soon as we have the lumber on the ground. We will probably have the shed pretty well finished by the end of next week. I will expect you to arrive with relief Saturday. I am not sure I can hold out much longer than that. [April 9, 1908]

Wilbur's diary entry for April 11 further described the damage:

. . . I learned from the men at the Station that the 1903 building was in fair shape till last Christmas except that the north end was undermined by the wind. The unsupported part swayed about till it went to pieces and finally a violent storm blew the balance of it down. . . . A few months ago some boys stopped at the camp and ripped the cloth on the 1902 surfaces and ripped up our cots. The floors of both buildings are a foot under the sand. Two of the carbide cans are still on hand somewhat rusted but not so badly as I would have expected. The pump is over at the Station but so badly rusted that it cuts out leathers as fast as they can be put in. Will order a new one ($3.00). Spent night at Kill Devil Station. The crew is as follows: Capt. J. E. Ward, Bob Wescott, W. S. Douglas, Uncle Benny O'Neal, W. O. Twifert, W. W. Midgett, Willis Tillett.

Wilbur arranged for Oliver O'Neal and others to help erect a new building. For the next couple of weeks, he met with various frustrations in trying to finish the structure before Orville arrived to begin assembling the Flyer. In a letter to his sister, Wilbur described the difficulties of getting lumber to the campsite.

We went back to the Sound and helped unload lumber the balance of the day. The big boat could not come nearer shore than 200 feet. It was necessary to transfer the lumber toward shore in small lots by means of a smaller boat and finally back a cart into the water till it was twenty or thirty feet from shore and make the final haul in still smaller lots. Saturday we went down with two carts and spent the day hauling the lumber to camp. Monday, with the assistance of two semi-carpenters, I began work on the new building and put in the foundation posts and part of the sills, but could not begin laying floor because only part of the joist had been brought down from Eliz. City. Sat. afternoon the *Lou Willis* tried to return to town for the balance of the lumber but had her sails blown off enroute and was compelled to return. It started again Monday and I am hopeful it may get back tonight. We were unable to do any more on the building today for lack of necessary material. The new building is to be 22 ft. wide and 48 ft. long so it is about a half larger than any we have used before. There will be plenty of room for kitchen, dining room, reception hall, parlor, and bedrooms, with bath accommodations, etc., etc., in one corner of the larger building. I do not think anything can be done to restore the old building now partly standing. [April 14, 1908]

A letter to his father two days later revealed Wilbur's mounting frustration:

This is my eleventh day from home and only one days work has been done on the new building. Two days were spent getting to Elizabeth City. Two were lost at Eliz. City waiting for the boat. One was spent on the sound enroute to Kitty Hawk. Friday and Saturday were spent selecting a location, landing and hauling lumber to it. Monday was spent putting in foundation and sills. Tuesday, Wednesday, and today, Thursday, have been spent in waiting for more lumber to arrive, and storms to pass. We hope to get down to work tomorrow. [April 16, 1908]

Two more days passed, and still not all of the lumber had arrived. Wilbur wrote in his diary:

Having failed in borrowing a cart, I started for Kitty Hawk on foot as soon as breakfast was over and saw Capt. Midgett. I proposed that he make a special trip to Eliz. City on the *Van Dusen* for our lumber. He and the boy did not like the idea, but finally consented to go for $20. I paid him the money and told him to go. It is a little hard having to pay for a special trip at a fancy price when he had made three trips without bringing anything. I suppose he was leaving the job for the sailboat. I returned by way of the Kitty Hawk station in order to send a telegram to the lumbermen to be sure to have the lumber at the wharf.

Reached camp about 11 o'clock having walked ten miles or more. The carpenters had finished putting in the sills and joist and were erecting studding. The *Lou Willis* came down and dumped the rest of the flooring ashore, and Aug Harris and

Spencer Midgett hauled it to camp. We were compelled to quit
work on account of rain, a little after 4 o'clock and were pretty
damp before we reached the Station. I have been bothered with
diarrhea for several days, due to the food we have, no doubt.
Conditions are almost intolerable. [Diary T, April 18, 1908]

Two days later Wilbur's diary records:

Owing to light wind *Lou Willis*, to which lumber was transferred,
did not get down the bay till eleven o'clock, thus keeping the
two carts idle all morning. After hauling one load Spencer
Midgett went home with headache without giving any chance to
me [to] get someone else. Harris hauled all afternoon. We got
up the rafters, and put down a little more than half the floor and
put siding on one side of building. I forgot to mention that we
noticed the gasoline barrel was smelling several days ago and
transferred what gasoline was left to the barrel left from previous trip. There was less than half a barrel of gasoline left.
Midgetts had thrown the barrel off the cart to unload it, and
sprung a leak. [April 20, 1908]

The next day:

Worked on the building all day. The floor is down and the side
walls finished. The north end is nearly done. One side of roof is
sheeted. If it is quiet we will get the paper on the roof tomorrow.
Paid Augustus Harris $9.00 for hauling & $1.00 to boy, who
came in Spencer Midgett's place, and sent bills of lading to
Capt. Midgett with $30.00 cash for freight charges on machine,
&c. [April 21, 1908]

And the following day, a Wednesday:

We finished the north end and finished sheeting the roof, and
have put the forty-foot strips of paper all on but two, when the
high wind made further work impossible. Started on the big
doors. [April 22, 1908]

On Thursday:

We finished putting paper on the roof, made and hung the big
doors and started the small doors, put in the south gable and a
few braces. Learned that Capt. Midgett has decided to make
only two trips this week. This will prevent us from receiving gasoline stove & groceries and will probably delay Orville's arrival.
[April 23, 1908]

Friday:

Finished the north doors and put on the outside braces. Made a
window in east wall. Found the gasoline barrel leaking badly and
moved it into the building out of the sun. Mr. Wescott brought
my trunk over from the station. The bill for carpenter work of
O'Neal and Baum, 6⅓ days, $22.20. Started to fix up kitchen
& beds. [April 24, 1908]

Saturday:

Chas. & I went over to camp with our suitcases, &c., and went to
work on tables & shelves for the kitchen. About ten o'clock

Harris & O'Neal arrived with two cartloads of flying machine freight and said Orville was at the old fish landing with the remainder. We went down and helped unload the big box and brought it to camp on long poles resting on two carts. Paid Midgetts $49.00 for freight & hotel. Also $26.00 for railroad frt. charges. Paid Harris & O'Neal $1.50 for hauling. Spent afternoon cleaning out trash and making the building inhabitable. I slept in a good bed of regular camp pattern. Orville slept on some boards thrown across the ceiling joist. Furnas slept on the floor. Each pronounced his own method a success.

[April 25, 1908]

Sunday, a day of rest:

Notwithstanding the success of the sleeping arrangements of Orville & Charley, they decided to make further improvements.

[April 26, 1908]

Finally, with the building finished, the brothers turned their attention to assembling the machine. They modified the 1905 Flyer by adding a thirty-five-horsepower engine with vertical instead of horizontal cylinders, a new arrangement of control levers, and seats for the pilot and passenger. In early May, they were ready to test the machine. Wilbur's diary records the first trial:

In the morning we took the machine out of the shed and tested putting on and removing the tail. By removing two bolts we can slip the rear tail & its framing forward till it does not extend beyond the screws. In this condition the machine can be run into the shed with the front rudder on. After dinner we took the machine to a point several hundred feet west of the building and prepared for a flight to the northwest, but the wind suddenly shifted to the north-northeast. Only a few minutes were required to shift the track to face the new wind direction. The track measured about 115 ft. No anemometer was fitted to the machine to record the distance traveled, and no record was made of the speed of the engine. A test of wind speed just before starting the engine for the flight showed $6\frac{1}{2}$ m. per sec. Another test about 20 minutes after the flight showed $3\frac{1}{2}$ m. per sec. The wind during the flight was probably 5 m. Distance over the ground was 1,008 ft. Time 22 seconds (O. W.). The machine was lifted after a run of not more than 95 ft., and at first had barely speed enough for flight, but it accelerated and at the end was probably going at least 35 miles over the ground and 45 through the air. The flight was very much up and down as the operator (W. W.) was thinking more of the side control than of the fore-and-aft control. The landing was made with the engine running and the machine inclined downward. The sand flew all over the machine. The cross-stick on which the little roller is mounted was broken, but otherwise no damage was done. Uncle Benny O'Neal and Willis Tillett were over from the Life Saving Station and helped bring back the machine.

[May 6, 1908]

Gradually, the brothers became more familiar with operating the new controls, and they increased the time and distance of their flights. Eight days later they added a new "first" to their list of achievements; they carried a passenger into the air. Charles Furnas, their helper from Dayton, had the honor of being the first person to fly as a passenger in a plane. Wilbur's diary recorded the event:

We began before eight o'clock with a flight with two men aboard (W. W. & C. F.). A good start was made but the course was soon directed more to the right than it should have been, and in order to keep on the safe side I had Chas. shut off the engine, as we were pointing right at the West Hill. The distance by anemometer was just 600 meters in 28³/₅ seconds. Easy landing.

Orville and Chas. tried a flight together and after one false start sailed away nicely. They passed around the West Hill, came north alongside the Little Hill by the sound, and back by way of starting point. When about halfway round the West Hill on the second lap, the heating of the engine bearing compelled them to land. I made a measurement of the wind shortly before they passed the building and found its velocity about 18 miles an hour. They say that at one time on the windward part of the course they met a gust that held them practically motionless for a few moments. . . .

The wind gradually shifted to the west and made starting more and more difficult. I made three attempts, with Chas. aboard, to get started but struck wing tips before reaching the end of the track. These false starts consumed most of the morning.

After dinner I tried alone with the track shifted more to the west and got off nicely. Skirting the north edge of the West Hill, I passed around the Little Hill by the sound and proceeded down the beach till I had passed the umbrella tree, then turned east and passed over the sand ridge about two hundred feet from its end. Then, turning southward, I passed over the dry ponds and, passing camp, proceeded around the West Hill and the Little Hill by the sound and was continuing the course followed on the first round when the machine suddenly darted into the ground when going with the wind at a velocity of about 85 kilometers an hour. The front framing and upper surface were wrecked. The front rudder & tail & machinery and the wing sections were almost intact. The lower center section was only slightly injured. I was thrown violently forward and landed against the top surface but remained inside the body of the machine. I received a slight cut across the bridge of my nose, several bruises on my left hand, right forearm, and both shoulders. The next day I felt a little stiff all over. I was practically uninjured. We tore the machine apart and put the lower surface on our trucks with the engine in place, and piled on the transmission & a few other parts, between four & five hundred pounds in all, and the three of us dragged it back to camp, a

distance of about a mile and a quarter. The heat had become almost unbearable and we barely escaped collapse before reaching the camp. After dark we went over and got the rudders and radiators. We went to bed completely fagged out.

[May 14, 1908]

In describing the incident to his sister Wilbur wrote, "I do not think the accident would have happened if we had not been so rushed and overworked."

Despite the unfortunate end to the day's trials, which also ended the 1908 practice session at Kill Devil Hills, the brothers were pleased. They had proved that they could meet the U.S. Army's requirements for a passenger machine. Furthermore, they had witnesses who could vouch for their achievements. News correspondents from several publications had come to the Kitty Hawk area to observe the Wrights from a distance, hoping to disprove the incredible rumors of a manned flying machine that were filtering into their home offices. To their amazement, the stories proved to be true. After seeing the passenger flight of May 14, one of the reporters, Byron Newton of the New York *Herald*, wrote in his diary: "Some day Congress will erect a monument here to these Wrights."

The wreck of the Flyer during the Kitty Hawk tests put even greater pressure on the Wrights in meeting their contracts. For the first time in their years of flying experiments, they had to go in separate directions. Wilbur left Kitty Hawk on May 17 to go directly to Europe, where he began assembling a Flyer for the demonstrations in France.

170

The Wrights returned to their camp at Kill Devil Hills in 1908 to find the buildings badly damaged. The remains of the 1902 glider are visible inside the wrecked building.

Orville left camp a few days later and returned to Dayton to begin building a new Flyer for the U.S. Signal Corps tests. By mid-September, almost simultaneously, the two brothers,—Wilbur at Camp d'Auvours, near Le Mans, France; and Orville at Fort Myer, Virginia—were dazzling the world with their feats. The Age of Flight had truly begun.

Went down to camp with little Spencer Midgett. Found things pretty well wrecked. The side walls of the old building still stand but the roof and the north end are gone. The new building is down and torn to pieces. The pump is gone. [Wilbur Wright's Diary T, April 10, 1908]

The older building suffered less damage than the 1903 building and provided shelter while the Wrights constructed new quarters for their Flyer.

Library of Congress

About noon I went over to the big hill and found the wind on top as high as 15 meters per sec. Measured height of hill and found it about 102 ft. The shape of the horns has apparently changed somewhat. Toward evening the wind swung around to S.E. and dropped to about 3 meters and later to two meters or less. The evening was beautiful, the moon being almost full. [Wilbur Wright's Diary T, April 12, 1908]

A portion of the Kill Devil Hills as photographed by the Wrights in 1908.

Took one photo of machine on the track before the first start. [Wilbur Wright's Diary T, May 11, 1908]

The remodeled 1905 Flyer, in the photograph mentioned in Wilbur's diary for May 11, 1908.

1911

A better knowledge of these air currents, so that one could keep his machine constantly in the rising trends, would enable one to remain aloft without power much longer than has yet been done. [Orville Wright to J.A. Heringa, November 18, 1911]

Eleven years after the Wrights had made their first trip to Kitty Hawk for gliding experiments, Orville took a new glider to the camp at Kill Devil Hills. Although the brothers were making rapid advances with powered Flyers, which by now were being manufactured and sold by the Wright Company in several countries, Orville wanted to test a new unpowered machine. Wilbur, since 1909 president of the company, remained behind to attend to other business, particularly their lawsuits against various patent infringers, while Orville and a British flight pioneer, Alec Ogilvie, went to Kitty Hawk. This was the last time either of the Wrights returned to the area for flying experiments.

Orville stayed at the camp from October 10 to October 30; during this time he made about 90 glides from the three hills of Kill Devil. Orville's new machine, a biplane with a 32-foot span and a wing area of 300 square feet, performed well under his skillful operation. On October 24, Orville set a world record for soaring flight—9 minutes and 45 seconds. His record stood unbeaten for a decade.

The Wright brothers had to pay a price for the success and fame they earned as a result of their achievements at Kitty Hawk and elsewhere. Other experimenters tried to dispute the brothers' claims to the originality of their machines; entrepreneurs tried to take advantage of them in their business dealings. In the midst of a long period of legal harassments, a tired Wilbur wrote:

During the past three months most of my time has been taken up with lawsuits and I have been away from home most of the time. I am hoping to be freed from this kind of work before another year has ended. It is much more pleasant to go to Kitty Hawk for experiments than to worry over lawsuits. We had hoped in 1906 to sell our invention to governments for enough money to satisfy our needs and then devote our time to science, but the jealousy of certain persons blocked this plan, and compelled us to rely on our patents and commercial exploitation. We wished to be free from business cares so that we could give all our own time to advancing the science and art of aviation, but we have been compelled to spend our time on business matters instead during the past five years. When we think what we might have accomplished if we had been able to devote this time to experiments, we feel very sad, but it is always easier to deal with things than with men, and no one can direct his life entirely as he would choose. [Wilbur Wright to William F. de Hevesy, January 25, 1912]

Wilbur never had the pleasure of returning to Kitty Hawk and his beloved experiments. On May 30, 1912, after an illness of several weeks, Wilbur succumbed to typhoid fever. He was forty-five years old — "a short life, full of consequences," Bishop Wright wrote in his diary that day.

Orville lived to be seventy-seven. He gave up piloting in 1918, but for many productive years he continued the inventive aeronautical work that he and Wilbur had begun.

Before his death in 1948, Orville witnessed dramatic world changes resulting from the technology that he and his brother had pioneered. He lived through two devastating world wars in which the Wright brothers' invention played a major role. He saw the jet engine replace the propeller. He saw airplanes whose wingspans were greater than the distance of the first flight; planes that could fly faster than the speed of sound. He saw centuries-old geographic barriers disappear and cultures mingle in defiance of space and time. He saw the inception of the Space Age and the harnessing of power that would thrust mankind beyond the bounds of Earth.

In November 1932, Orville returned to Kitty Hawk to visit the site where, fifteen years earlier, he and his brother had introduced this liberating technology to the world. He was present for the dedication of a national monument to their achievements. Inscribed in the base of the sixty-foot granite pylon, appropriately topped with a beacon, were these words of tribute to their work:

In commemoration of the conquest of the air by the brothers Wilbur and Orville Wright. Conceived by genius. Achieved by dauntless resolution and unconquerable faith.

Beyond the memorial at the Kill Devil Hills, the world pays tribute to the Wright brothers' legacy with continuing advances in flight and space technology. In 1969, when Neil Armstrong landed Apollo 11 on the moon and took his giant step "for all mankind," he brought with him a piece of the original fabric from the Wright Flyer that had made history at Kitty Hawk, North Carolina, on that windy day in December, 1903.

177

Orville gliding over the camp at Kill Devil Hills in 1911.

Arrived at Kill Devil. Worked on buildings & fittings. (Rained night.)
[Orville Wright's Diary V, October 10, 1911]

The new glider, parked in front of a camp building in 1911.

Wright State University

178

Measured West Hill = 80 ft. high [Slope] 500 ft. Kill Devil Hill =
[slope] 665 [ft. at] 8°40' = 103 ft. high. 30-mile wind at top hill.
18 on ground. [Orville Wright's Diary V, October 12, 1911]

Big Kill Devil Hill, photographed when Orville returned in 1911, eleven years after the Wrights first began their gliding experiments.

Library of Congress

West Hill: 3 glides. Shot up at landing and dropped about 6 feet, bending rear center uprights. Horizontal rudder too small. Vert. rudder too small (7½ ft. area, 7 ft. in rear of back edge of surface). Put on a vane on front upright. Vane was one of rear rudder planes of 1905 machine, 18" X 6'.

Kill Devil Hill: After one glide, in which I pitched forward out of machine, put on large rudder, 38" X 8'10", using center of 1905 rudder. Afterward made glide of 637 ft. in curved line, [plus] 586 ft. in straight line. Angle 7°45'. Wind very light (4 mi.). Time 23 seconds.

[Orville Wright's Diary V, October 16, 1911]

Carrying the glider back to the launch site, 1911.

180

Many thanks for your congratulations on our work with the glider at Kitty Hawk. Flying in a 25 meter per second wind is no snap, and I can tell you that it keeps one pretty busy with the levers. I got caught in one whirl of wind that turned my machine completely around and drove me into the hill. I didn't receive a scratch, but the machine needed the doctor pretty badly. I found that in order to fly in such winds a greater control than has ever been put on any power machine would be necessary. It was not the velocity of the wind, but its sudden changes in direction that made the flying difficult. . . .

A rather amusing incident happened when we were at Kitty Hawk last month. It seems that Montgomery was doing some gliding in California at the same time that we were experimenting at Kitty Hawk. Evidently he was not doing anything that had the least appearance of soaring, for, when the report went forth that I had remained in the air for nearly ten minutes without the use of any artificial power, one of Montgomery's staunch supporters, Victor Loughead, went all the way down to our camp in order that he could "set us right before the world." When he learned at first-hand from a half dozen different persons who had been eyewitnesses of the flights that the reports were really true, he skipped out without ever even seeing the machine! On his first appearance he told the reporters that he knew we must have been misrepresented in the reports, since it would be utterly impossible to remain aloft five minutes without the use of artificial power.

[Orville Wright to Capt. Thomas S. Baldwin, November 18, 1911]

Orville soaring in the 1911 glider on one of his record-breaking flights.

In regard to the experiments which I lately made in soaring flight, in many of which flights I remained in the air for periods of three to five minutes, and in one flight for a space of nine and three quarter minutes, I will say that this kind of flight, though never before achieved by man, is very common with birds in southern countries, some of which can remain in the air for hours at a time without the expenditure of any muscular power. Of course I do not mean to say that in absolutely calm air, or in air having an absolutely horizontal direction, it would be possible to fly without the expenditure of artificial power, but as the air is never absolutely calm, and as it flows with upward and downward trends, by taking advantage of the former, it is possible to use the power of the upward trend of the air, and thus dispense with all artificial power.

[Orville Wright to J. A. Heringa, November 18, 1911]

*Orville soaring. The men
on the ground are not
saluting his performance;
they're holding their hats in
a high wind.*

188

Selections of Wright material for this book were drawn primarily from original letters, diaries, and notebooks in the Wright collections at the Library of Congress and from the two volumes of *The Papers of Wilbur and Orville Wright, Including the Chanute-Wright Letters and Other Papers of Octave Chanute*, edited by Marvin W. McFarland (New York: McGraw-Hill, 1953; reprint ed., New York: Arno Press, 1972). Two other published books, *Miracle at Kitty Hawk: The Letters of Wilbur and Orville Wright*, edited by Fred C. Kelly (New York: Farrar, Straus, and Young, 1951); and Harry Combs, *Kill Devil Hill: Discovering the Secret of the Wright Brothers* (Boston: Houghton Mifflin, 1979), were important references.

Reproductions of original photographs were obtained from the Wright Brothers Collection, Wright State University, Dayton, Ohio; the Wilbur and Orville Wright Collection, Prints and Photographs Division, Library of Congress; and the Wright Brothers Documentary Research Files, National Air and Space Museum, Smithsonian Institution.

189

Library of Congress